M000032098

# Table of Contents

In loving memory of my dear deceased son, Stephen (Steve),
who died suddenly on October 18, 2021. In this picture,
Steve and Jean are attending the wedding of his daughter
Brooke to Brian Gillespie. Photo by Sheketa Daniels, Steve's wife.

# How Did I Get Here?

## *The Force Within*

## Jean Bryant

How Did I Get Here?
*The Force Within*
Copyright © 2022 by Jean Bryant. All Rights Reserved.

For more information about this title contact the publisher
at jeanbryant@comcast.net

ISBN: 978-0-578-30167-9 (Paperback)

Printed in the United States of America

Cover and Interior design: Van-garde Imagery

Front Cover Photo by Elizabeth A. Roach
Back Cover Photo by Annette Banks

# Dedication

THIS BOOK IS DEDICATED TO my beloved mother, Nettie E. Williams. now deceased, who loved and supported me through triumphs and failures, through thick and thin. Her love knew no boundaries. Her kindness and compassion were wonderful characteristics, hopefully imbedded in me by her example.

It is also dedicated to the memory of my four beloved sons Crawford, Stephen, Bernard and Charles, all now deceased and sorely missed, who often shared my love for them with others as I followed God's plan for me.

My book is dedicated as well to my sisters, Elizabeth (Betty) and Sarah and Sarah's sons Daniel, Ronald and his wife, Susan and their daughter, Larisa.

Also, to my grandchildren, Andiaye, Keisha, Khadijah, Terri, Daralyn, Brooke, Taylor and Stephen C., and to my Staten Island family members, including Jenny Smith, Paulette Rhodes and the Briggs and Fish families. And to step-sons, Thomas, Richard (Kip,) and Kenneth (Juice) Bryant and the entire Bryant family.

# Foreword

*by Carolyn V. Callahan*

DRIVEN BY A 'CAN DO' spirit, nourished by her mother, Jeanette "Jean" Marie Roach was destined for success. In 1943, Jean, 11, and her twin sister Betty took a city bus ride from their family home in Roselle, New Jersey to New York City where they gained access to The Mills Brothers, a famous American jazz and traditional pop vocal quartet. Jean and Betty planned to broker a deal with the quartet to sing songs written by the sisters. The quartet did not listen to their "sales pitch," advising the sisters to return another day. The sisters never met the quartet again, but the journey to success had begun.

*How Did I Get Here?* is Jean's story. The pages are inclusive of obstacles, successes, and illustrative career experiences.

An impressionable child, Jean grew up in church where she loved hearing stories about Jesus and his goodness. The impact of Sunday services grew along with Jean into adulthood.

In 1963, Jean Daniels, now the married mother of four, agreed to manage her son Stephen's eight-piece all male band, The Soul Dukes. She was not deterred by inexperience or being a woman in a male dominated profession. Jean's innate organization and management skills did not go unnoticed. Impressed by the band, following a performance, advertising executive George Hudson asked Stephen who managed the band. When he replied my mother, Hudson said tell her to call me. Jean's phone call led to three lucrative years of employment with the advertising agency, ending after Hudson passed. The advertising experience led to an amazing 29-year career in journalism with the New Jersey Afro-American Newspaper (1970-1971), Pittsburgh Press (1972-1993) and Pittsburgh Post-Gazette (1993-1999). Jean gained a reputation as "the reporter who always got a story." In telling her story, Jean also proudly writes about her four unique sons.

By 1972 Jean Bryant, newly remarried, was residing in Pittsburgh, Pennsylvania. Jean's 'can do' spirit led to the establishment of two annual eight-week self-improvement programs for youth, the Miss Black Teenage Pageant (1973-2008) and the Mister African American program (1993-2002). The programs inspired more than 2,000 teenagers ages 10 to 17 to face life challenges by always wearing their CAP (Confidence, Awareness, and Pride).

In Pittsburgh, Jean also found time to be an active organizer and community leader. Since 1974, she has received distinguished awards in communications and journalism excellence, community and humanitarian service, youth motivation, achievement and empowerment, women of excellence and achievement, and fashion. She also has earned city, county, and state government citations for her contributions to society. She also has been the honoree of several "legacy" ceremonies. The film, *Crowning Achievement*, features Jean's work with youth. The production won an Emmy: Historic/Cultural Program Feature Section (February 2020) and the Pennsylvania Association of Broadcasters Award (February 2021) as well as a golden Quill Award.

# Preface

As I reflect on my journey through life, I am in wonderment, in awe that I accomplished so much against so many odds.

I realize *I was never alone. Not for a minute. God was always there.* Always moving me forward. *He* was that force within me. *He* was the driving force that kept me going when others were doubtful.

For the many awards bestowed upon me for the Miss Black Teenage and Mister African American programs and for my journalistic work, I give the glory to God.

I am grateful for the MBT/MAA Committee members who stood beside me and shared my vision for 35 years as well as for the parents who entrusted their precious children to our care.

The young women – 1,891 in number; the young men about 200 in number – were all a blessing to me. And I pray I was, in some way, a blessing to them.

As for the many stories I've written during my career as a journalist, God guided my every thought. All the glory and honor I give to Him.

I Hope all who read this book will be encouraged to look back on their lives as I have done and see how God is always with them. Then, praise Him mightily.

# ashion Week events draw SRO crowds

Julia Rendleman/Post-Gazette

Pittsburgh Fashion Hall of Fame inductees for 2013: Tom Julian, left; Jean Bryant, third from left; Debbie Norrell, right; exceptional artist awardee Jacqueline Capatolla, second from left.

festivities will be Tall Cathy from 96.1 KISS and Sheri Van Dyke of 94.5 3WS. Doors open at 7 p.m. Tickets are available at all Philip Pelusi Salon locations.

**Dress for Success Pittsburgh "fill a bag" sale returns:** From 9 a.m. to 3 p.m. through Thursday, grab bargains on suits, separates, outerwear and more. For $20, shoppers will receive a bag they can stuff with as much apparel as they can. Dress for Success Pittsburgh is at the Warner Centre, 332 Fifth Ave., 5th floor, Downtown. Information: 412-201-4204.

**Trunk shows for him at Larrimor's:** Infuse

his professional attire with Italian craftsmanship and class with suits and sportswear from Ermenegildo Zegna. Polish off the ensemble with handcrafted shoes from the third-generation family-owned brand, Magnanni. Both will be in the Downtown store on Thursday. Information: 412-471-5727 or www.larrimors.com.

**Free scarf Fridays, Rubber Duck merchandise at Fifth Avenue Place, Downtown:** Spend $10 or more at Laurie's Hallmark, upper level, on Fridays in October and receive a free fashion scarf in a variety of colors and designs.

Also stop by WelcomePittsburgh on the lower level to shop official Rubber Duck Project merchandise, in honor of the river exhibit on display as part of the Pittsburgh Cultural Trust's Pittsburgh International Festival of Firsts. Information: www.fifthavenueplacepa.com.

**Claire la Faye bridal trunk show:** For brides-to-be seeking a nontraditional look for their wedding day, browse whimsical-yet-modern and edgy dresses at a trunk show Friday through Sunday at Glitter & Grit, 5300 Butler St., Lawrenceville. Call 412-781-2375 or visit www.glitterandgritpgh.com.

**Clothing swap at Physique Rx'd pilates:** Spruce up your wardrobe for fall — without spending a lot — at the second House of Colour Pittsburgh free clothing swap from noon to 5 p.m. Sunday at 910 Galveston Ave., North Side.

Personal color and style consultant Julie Peterson will help women pick pieces that work best for their complexion and colorings. Plus, direct sales jeweler Stella & Dot will be on hand with fresh accessories for the season. Unwanted clothes will be donated to Dress for Success. Information: www.houseofcolour.co.uk/juliepeterson.

**White House | Black Market opens at Mall at Robinson:** Ladies seeking modern apparel with sophisticated style now can check out the 3,000-square-foot boutique on the lower level near Banana Republic. Through Oct. 27, shoppers will receive an in-store offer for $20 off a full-price purchase of at least $80.

**Grove City Premium Outlets to recognize Breast Cancer Awareness Month:** Through October, shoppers can visit the onsite information center to donate $10 to Susan G. Komen for the Cure. Each donation of at least $10 will be awarded savings cards worth 25 percent off a single item at select stores.

*For more from PG fashion writer Sara Bauknecht, check out the PG's Stylebook blog at www.post-gazette.com/stylebook. Follow her on Twitter @SaraB_PG. To have a fashion or style event considered for Stylebook, send listing to sbauknecht@post-gazette.com.*

Chapter One:

# The Force

THE DATE WAS SEPT. 29, 2013. I was 81 years old and being presented with an award as one of six inductees in the Pittsburgh, PA Fashion Hall of Fame.

I had agonized for two days over what to wear for the occasion. Should I wear my red pants suit with my 12-tail fox stole? No. Instead, I chose to wear a unique glittering multi-colored sequined jacket over black satin pants. I was happy I chose to wear the sequined Jacket. I got many compliments.

At home that night, I pondered, how I, a shy, small-town girl from Roselle, New Jersey wound up in the Pittsburgh Fashion Hall of Fame?

More significantly, it was the *third award* in a year's time since I celebrated my 80th birthday July 1, 2012 at the Sheraton Hotel's Fountainview Room, overlooking the Monongahela River. On that day, 106 guests helped me celebrate more than 40 years of living in Pittsburgh's Steel City.

That was one of the happiest days of my life and well worth the money spent. The money was part of an inheritance from my mother. She loved to entertain and would have loved the setting – chandeliers glittering like diamonds overhead, soft music playing, guests happily chattering. I only wished she had lived to be there. I know in my heart she would have approved.

Leading up to the Pittsburgh Fashion Hall of Fame award, I'd received the 2012 New Pittsburgh Courier's 50 Women of Excellence *Legacy* Award (in 2008, I was one of 50 recipients of its Women of Excellence Award); followed in March with the National Council of Negro Women's Legacy Award and finally The Pittsburgh Fashion Hall of Fame.

How is this happening, I asked myself. What Force is moving me? Is it God? I wondered. Why am I so blessed?

From that time on, I began to ponder my life more earnestly, wondering about the circumstances that led me to this life: What Force pushed me, with only a GED, to playing a significant role in helping to elect Orange, New Jersey's *first* black councilman, Benjamin Jones? I was just a housewife in that small town. How did that happen?

As Chair of the Citizens for Representative Government's Women's Division to Elect Ben Jones, I knocked on every door and talked to each voter! With that amazing win, I suddenly realized I had the ability to persuade others in ways beyond my ability to understand at that moment.

*So many questions came to mind after that pivotal event. What Force is moving me? Where did this skill and drive originate?*

And how was it that I, a young mother of four sons, could be so convincing? How was it that I – who was raised in a strict *fire and brimstone- speak-only-when-spoken to Baptist family* – could muster the courage and words to change minds and sway the obstinate. How could I eventually become a writer for major newspapers, using words that would bring professional awards?

Did this powerful energy become unleashed when I became a saleswoman for a china and crystal company? What Force enabled me to take my son's band from a four-piece group practicing in our living room to becoming an eight-piece band performing locally and as far away as the French Riviera?

Press Release

Pittsburgh Fashion Week
P.O. Box 17947
Pittsburgh, PA 15235-7947

**Pittsburgh Fashion Week**

For Immediate Release #2
May 6, 2013

Presents the Fourth Annual Induction of Fashion Icons

## Pittsburgh Fashion Hall of Fame 2013

**(Pittsburgh, Pa)** – The votes are in and *Pittsburgh Fashion Week* is delighted to announce the fourth year of nominees for induction to the *Pittsburgh Fashion Hall of Fame 2013.*

The honoree's qualification is based upon their unique, outstanding, and long-term contribution to fashion, style and beauty in Southwestern Pennsylvania. This distinction is bestowed by *Pittsburgh Fashion Week* and will occur annually during the weeklong event.

**The Honorees:**

Michael Barone – Creative Director of MODA Men's Fashions

Jean Bryant – Retired Journalist for Pittsburgh Post Gazette and Founder of "Miss Black Teenage Program" & "Mr. African American Programs"

Tom Julian – Fashion Expert & Author of Nordstrom's Guide to Men's Style

Debbie Norrell – Lifestyle Editor for the "New Pittsburgh Courier"

EB Pepper – Owner of EB Pepper

Marianne Skiba – Emmy Award Winning Celebrity Makeup Artist

**"Exceptional Artist Award"**

Jacqueline Capatolla – Entrepreneur, Owner/Artist of JACQUELINE'S Salon & Author of 'Shear Dreams'

What Force would lead me to manage a radio advertising agency, bringing in thousands of dollars with my ideas?

No doubt, this same Force led me 400 miles away from Orange – a community about 2.2 square miles in area – to Pittsburgh in 1972, then the fifth largest corporate city in America. This was the city where 1,891 young women and 200 young men would eventually be guided by programs I formulated, produced and directed. These young men and women would become doctors, lawyers, entertainers, scholars, law enforcement officers and businessmen and women. Some were recipients of the more than $500,000 in educational scholarships from my programs.

And it boggles my mind that on February 20, 2020, a documentary, *"A Crowning Achievement,"* produced by WQED'S digital Producer, Annette Banks, about my work with the two youth programs – Miss Black Teenage and Mister African American – would win an Emmy! Several months later it won a second award from The Pennsylvania Broadcasters Association. A third award – a Golden Quill – followed still later.

*I've come to realize that this Force guiding me, moving me from within was God himself. He saw something in me that He could use to touch others, to bring about a change, no matter how small. I feel humbled and blessed by the love and attention He has shown me.*

Chapter Two:
# Who Am I?

ON JULY 1, 1932, I was born, Jeanette Marie (Jean) Roach, with an identical twin, Elizabeth Anne (Betty) in St. Vincent's Hospital, Staten Island, New York. Our twin births came as a complete surprise to our parents Nettie Elizabeth Burdette, of Roselle, N. J. and Chomondeley de Ravenna Roach, a native of Trinidad, who was living in New York City.

Named after her mother, young Nettie was a beautiful, softspoken woman, who grew up in a very strict and traditional home in Roselle. Her mother (our grandmother) was Nettie Fish – a native of Brooklyn, N. Y., and a descendant of New York's Shinnecock Indian Tribe. Her father (our grandfather) was Bernard Manon Burdette, a carpenter by trade and a native of Burdett, N. Y., a village settled by his English ancestors.

Nettie Fish was the family matriarch. She married twice. Her first marriage to Thomas Wilmore yielded four sons and a daughter, Wilhelmina. Her second marriage to Bernard Burdette resulted in the birth of our mother, Nettie Elizabeth.

The elder Nettie was a fierce but kind, religious woman, who ruled the roost. No one dared to speak negatively or disagree with her. She was known in our community as "Mom Burdette."

I remember how Mom Burdette's sons Samuel, Philip, Charles and George Wilmore faithfully paid tribute to their mother early

Sunday mornings with envelopes of money as their wives tagged along with freshly baked goods, rolls, cakes and pies.

According to a story handed down to us, young Nettie was an excellent student. She was able to graduate a year early from Abraham Clark High School and was awarded a scholarship to an out-of-state college. But her parents, a product of their times, believed it would be improper for a young woman to live away from home until she was married. Pursuing a career as a single woman was out of the question. Men in the family, on the other hand, were accomplished. They would achieve success in various professional endeavors.

Chomondeley, a violinist, met my mother in Staten Island. N.Y. through mutual friends. They had a common interest in tennis and enjoyed playing together on local tennis courts. They fell in love and married, taking up residence in Staten Island. But six months after our birth, my mother fled the marriage, claiming her husband was too controlling.

Nettie Elizabeth and her twins settled in with her parents, who were living in one of the homes owned by the elder Nettie's son, Samuel, on East Eighth Avenue in Roselle.

East Eighth Avenue was a quiet street on which older two-story wood-frame homes lined one side of the street. Across the street, newer two-story red-brick homes replaced wooded acreage that once grew there. It was a middle-class neighborhood of black-owned homes, a safe neighborhood, alive with children playing hop-scotch, marbles, ball games, weather permitting.

Four of the homes on that street were owned by my mother's step-brothers: Samuel Wilmore owned two of the homes, and Philip and Charles Wilmore each owned one of the other two. The four homes stood side by side. (A fourth step-brother, George Wilmore, resided in a home he owned in Newark, N. J.)

We lived in Samuel's house with seven other family members, including our grandparents, Nettie and Bernard, and Cousins Gladys and Mildred, Aunt Wilhelmina and her two sons, Cousins Walter and Eddie.

It was a warm and loving extended family. We did not seem crowded at all. There was no squabbling. Everyone knew their place. The women kept the kitchen clean and washed clothes. The men disappeared into the living room or their bedrooms.

How comforting it was to be surrounded by such a loving close-knit family as we grew up.

I remember how much we, her twin daughters, adored our mother. There was a special quality about her, something ethereal. She exuded a quiet grace. She was soft spoken, gentle, kind. She never spoke a harsh word against anyone. And she never lifted her voice or a hand to her children. My mother was a wonderful cook and loved to share her culinary talents with others by entertaining friends. They flocked to her parties knowing they would enjoy good food in a warm setting. I always wished I could be like her someday.

The memories of those innocent times are so heart-warming, so special to me: being serenaded by Cousin Eddie and his teen friends outside our home. They went around the neighborhood in Roselle, harmonizing Doo Wop. One of them – Tony Williams – rose to fame in the 1940s as lead singer for the Platters. However, not everyone was appreciative of the melodious sounds emanating from the young songsters.

From her second story window Old Lady Scott would spew her own kind of venom at them: "Go away or I'll call the cops," she would threaten any time they approached her corner building at Ninth Avenue and Spruce Street.

There were sweeter memories of Cousin Mildred coming home each night from her work in a laundry with pastries from a local bakery. But best of all memories were feeling the warmth of our mother's hugs when she came home each evening from her secretarial job at Book-of-the-Month Club in New York City.

Betty and I are mirror twins. We have the same markings on our bodies, but on opposite sides. And our personalities are opposite as well. I tend to be shy, reserved; Betty is bold, self-assured.

As twins were such a rarity, Betty and I were doted upon by our entire family. We were spoiled, rarely spanked for mischievousness, not even when we scribbled large "murals" on the hallway wall leading upstairs to our bedrooms.

One "mural" depicted a milkman and his horse complete with droppings! Needless to say, that "mural" had a short life.

But one annoyance for us was the constant comparisons others made between us. The decisions usually went like this: "Betty is the beautiful one, Jean is the cute one."

What were people thinking when such comments were made in front of us?

I never realized the impact those comparisons would have until later in life when Betty and I were shopping in Downtown Elizabeth. She asked me, "Jean, why do you always smile at your reflection in store windows when we're out?" There I was standing at a store-front display window doing exactly that, smiling.

I had no answer then, and had not realized I did that. I came to believe the comparisons thoughtlessly made between us as children caused such an insecurity in me that I began checking to see if I was indeed cute. I worked hard to correct that habit.

Our creative juices began to flow in our pre-teen years. I began to write lyrics of love, love lost and unrequited love. I was too young to be tackling such subjects, and am not sure what served as my inspiration. I also wrote my first "novel" when I was eight years-old. I trashed it after I caught my Cousin Gladys reading it. Perhaps I was embarrassed that someone discovered what I had written, which I considered very private.

She apologized and said she just couldn't put it down. I don't remember now what I wrote back then and I wish I hadn't acted so rashly. But I couldn't escape the writing bug. My attention turned to song.

I couldn't read music and had no training in writing songs, still I dreamed that one day I would get my lyrics in the hands of a big-name star who would write music for those lyrics and record them. Of course, the songs would be hits.

So, when I learned one particular day in 1943 that the nationally popular singing quartet – The Mills Brothers – would be appearing at a theater in nearby New York City, I was ecstatic. The Mills Brothers were famous throughout the late 1930s and 1940s for their extraordinary harmony. Their play list was comprised of jazz, pop, and gospel.

This is my chance! This is what I've been waiting for!" I thought.

I emptied my piggy bank, and convinced Betty to accompany me to the theater where the famous group was appearing. Unbeknownst to family, we slipped off to the Big Apple on a New York-bound bus to see them. I hoped the 45-minute ride would not be in vain, that once they read my lyrics they would consider recording them.

It was a Saturday afternoon. We arrived at the theater between shows and knocked on what turned out to be the back stage door. The Mills Brothers held court with us at the door. We were not invited inside. The group seemed to be collectively amused at the appearance of such precocious 11- year-olds. However, they listened politely, patiently as we boldly explained our mission.

But the enthusiasm I had for my artistic endeavors didn't meet with the results I anticipated. Instead of jumping at the chance to put my beautiful lyrics to music and song, the group members nonchalantly cited their need to think things over and suggested that we might return the following Monday – a school day – to further discuss things.

I knew we could not return. We had already risked punishment for this one misadventure. My dreams were dashed. My young mind hadn't comprehended the legal steps involved in such transactions. We rode the bus back to Jersey quietly. I could tell Betty felt my disappointment. We never went back and I sadly put my folder of lyrics way.

In 1943, Our mother married a second time. Daniel Solon Pinkett, also a Roselle resident, had studied pharmacy but was unable to find employment in that field. So, he took a job at New York City's main post office. My youngest sister, Sarah Marian, was born of that union in 1945.

All of us had fun while our mother dated Daniel. Betty and I looked forward to the Sunday afternoon rides in his old model Hudson, a product of the old Hudson Motor Car Company in Detroit, Michigan. The rides wound leisurely through nearby

Warinanco Park, and were always topped- off with a stop at a popular ice cream parlor. We happily anticipated double dipped ice cream cones in our favorite flavors. It was a glorious time. After dating for several months, our mother and Daniel announced their engagement. We were happy. Our mother was radiant, in love.

Suddenly, however, the happy music stopped for me. The wedding, a simple affair, took place at Daniel's home on Seventh Avenue in Roselle, where the blissful couple would live. Shortly after their marriage, and without discussion, we twins were moved in with Daniel and our mother.

Our young minds hadn't thought that far ahead. I felt betrayed, as only a child can feel in this instance. We had always had our mother to ourselves. Suddenly, we were sharing my beautiful mother with Daniel Pinkett. (We were still calling him Mr. Pinkett). Emotions I didn't understand were churning inside me. I began to act out, sulking, not doing my chores when it was my turn.

One Saturday, after being *rightfully* punished for my rebellious ways, I found my way to a friend's dormitory room at a nearby nursing school.

Marjorie Briggs was the older sister of my best friend, Marian. Their father was a well-known construction engineer and owned his own business. Marjorie was at once surprised and distressed to find me standing at the door to her dormitory room.

She listened patiently to my story. "You can't stay here too long," Marjorie chided me "I could get in trouble."

Then, like the big sister she was, Marjorie imparted Big Sister Wisdom, lecturing me on why I should abandon my selfish thinking, realize the love my mother and Daniel had for me and allow *their love for each other* to flourish as well.

Marjorie called my mother, told her that she would allow me to stay overnight and that she would send me home in the morning. By the time I got home, however, a crisis had occurred. Daniel had suddenly taken ill and was rushed off to the hospital, where a few hours later, he died. What he died of was never discussed with us. I suspect it was cancer, a subject only spoken about in hushed tones back then. Even as I experienced cancer later in life at age 50, it was treated as a secret to be kept to one's self.

Now, my mother was a widow woman and baby Sarah was fatherless. Until his funeral, I never saw Daniel again. I never got the chance to apologize for my disobedience. Worse yet, I never got to say good bye, something that would haunt me for years.

# Chapter Three:

# Growing Up

GROWING UP IN ROSELLE, MY sisters and I attended Chestnut Elementary School. Teachers there became suspicious when my twin and I had identical answers on almost every test. They tried seating us as far away from each other as possible. It didn't work. Our answers were still similar, virtually the same.

It apparently didn't occur to them that we lived and breathed the same air. Why wouldn't our test papers bear similarities?

Overall, those years at Chestnut and later at Abraham Clark High School were fun and the teachers were great.

In Ninth grade, Betty and I decided to play an April Fool's Day trick on our teachers. Betty's class was studying algebra, while my class was studying French. So, we switched classes.

While some students could tell the difference between us, our teachers could not. So, we were sure our trick would work.

I was a star student in Mister Bauer's French class – so much so that I aced every test and rarely scored less than an "A" on assignments. Betty, however, was completely lost when Mr. Bauer – *thinking Betty was me* – called on her.

When she couldn't answer his question, the class howled uproariously, which angered Mr. Bauer no end. After all, he had constantly reminded his class that "If it wasn't for Jeanette, I would think I was a bad teacher!"

And now, those in the class who could tell the difference between Betty and me, were laughing because "Jeanette" couldn't answer a question.

In the meantime, math teacher Mr. Murphy, a good-natured red head, with a generous sized belly, called on me (posing as Betty). My failure to answer the question brought chuckles that annoyed Mr. Murphy. When the chuckles became louder, Mr. Murphy demanded to know what was going on. "Class what *is* the matter?" he asked. When the laughter became louder, he closed his book and stared into the class, looking to find a clue. Suddenly, his belly was moving up and down as he began to get the joke. Since all eyes were on me, he finally realized *I was not Elizabeth.*

*April Fool!*

Mother & daughters: seated: Sarah and Mother
Nettie. Standing L to R: Jean and Betty

Outside Mr. Murphy's classroom door, Betty was peeking to see if it was safe. Mr. Murphy, still laughing, waved her in.

"Mr. Murphy, I don't know a bit of French." Betty cried.

Meanwhile, when I returned to Mr. Bauer's French class, he was still unaware of the joke. When I walked in, there was more laughter and I could see how angry Mr. Bauer was. I was prompted to ask, "Mr. Bauer, didn't anybody *tell* you?"

"Tell me what?" he demanded. "That was my sister, Elizabeth!" I answered. His face turned crimson red as he tried unsuccessfully to stifle his own laughter.

It was a gag that reverberated throughout the school that day, one which had never been done in the school's history, we were told.

Also, in ninth grade, I experienced my first (psychological) bullying when a particular classmate – to whom I shall refer to as "My Bully" – showed me a guest list for her upcoming party. Neither my name or my twin's name was on that "elite" list of kids from my neighborhood. It's a slight I found hard to forget. I felt humiliated, sad.

My Bully was not done yet. She later presented me with a guest list to peruse for *another* party. "Of course, Betty and I will be invited to *this* party." But no. You guessed it. Our names were not on *that* list either. For me, the hurt lasted for some time. However, it didn't seem to matter to Betty at all. She was not so bothered by the slight.

I do believe that, in some ways, the bullying made me a better person. As an adult, I am particularly sensitive to the feelings of others, a trait that would reveal itself in many of the stories I wrote as a journalist and as a producer of programs for young males and females. All of which brought me county, state and community awards.

I did not graduate from Abraham Clark High School. I dropped out to marry Crawford Daniels and eventually raise four Sons. I earned my GED at Barringer Evening High School in Newark, N. J., where I fared so well on tests, the teacher later said to me, "You really don't *need* to be here. If you want, I'll be glad to sign your graduation certificate now. It's up to you." I happily accepted my early graduation.

**L to R, Jean, Nettie, Baby Sarah, Betty**

My twin Betty graduated in 1950 from Abraham Clark High School, where she was ranked in the top percentile of her class.

She went on to the University of Wisconsin, where she majored in English and the Humanities. After graduating from Wisconsin U. in 1954, she became much sort after because of her expertise and went on to teach English and Latin at Rockford West High School in Rockford, Ill. After three years, she followed her dream to live abroad and moved to Oslo, Norway, where she taught English and Latin at Oslo American high school. She later retired from teaching to open a bakery that featured American pastries.

Now, fully retired, Betty still enjoys life in that Nordic Country.

After graduating from Abraham Clark High School, our sister, Sarah, attended the Ophelia de Vore School of Charm in New York City, where she graduated in 1964. She later became an Executive Secretary for Macy's Federated Department Stores Corporation, a job she held for the next 20 years. Sarah is the mother of two sons, Daniel Fletcher and Ronald Fletcher, husband of Susan Fletcher

On April 8, 2000, Betty attended her first high school class reunion. Sarah and I joined her. The reunion was held at the Kenilworth Hotel, near Roselle.

Betty and I had taken great care to dress to the nines for the occasion. I wore a Nolan Miller outfit. He is known for his designs for the likes of actress Joan Collins and singer/actress Cher. My Nolan Miller was a pink dress suit. The shoulders of the jacket were drenched in crystal beads. My 12-tail fox stole was draped over my right shoulder, with the tails stretching to my ankle. Betty wore a classic black pinstriped dress suit with a silver fox stole adorning her right shoulder.

Sarah ran ahead with her camera to capture our entrance into the ballroom. This is Sarah's description of that moment:

Mother Nettie                 Sister Sarah

"The room was abuzz with everyone engaged in conversation. But when you and Betty entered the ballroom together, the buzz stopped. You could hear a pin drop!"

My Bully was in attendance and stared at me most of the evening, mouth agape, clearly stunned that this apparently well-to-do vision of success was the same person she had so gleefully humiliated back in the day. Each time, I looked in her direction, she was staring at me with incredulity.

My reaction? Smiles, just smiles.

*The Force had taken care of things in more ways than one.*

Mother Nettie, Betty and Sarah with Cousin Eddie

Mother Nettie in Norway

The reunion booklet listed our bios. I was recorded as an award-winning journalist for the Pittsburgh Press, largest newspaper in Western Pennsylvania and as the producer of a self-improvement program for young women and an anti-violence program for young men, with local, and state government awards for community service.

Betty was listed as a retired teacher living in Europe (Norway) and the owner of The Upper Crust, an American bakery, one of the first of its kind in Europe.

I couldn't help noticing My Bully's bio. It listed nothing of note, no community service.

*Here was that force, bringing me to this time and place.*

It had been years, since I had been humiliated by My Bully. I arrived at the reunion thinking only of the joy of seeing old classmates again. Now, I felt an inner triumph. I was, perhaps, one of the most successful females in the room of mostly teachers, and several doctors. For I had, in so many ways, impacted the lives of, perhaps, as many children as these professionals through my writings and my two programs – Miss Black Teenage (1,891) and Mister African American (200). My programs not only inspired educational pursuit but helped many youngsters financially by awarding many of them cash scholarships to the tune of approximately $500,000 over a period of 35 years,

*So, I never expected this sudden feeling of victory over a long-ago humiliation. I had not sought it.*

In full disclosure, I must admit that during the reunion, I was reminded by a former male classmate that *I* had, in fact, bullied *him*. He joined a group in which I was standing, remembering good times.

"Remember how you beat me up, Jean," he interjected to my extreme embarrassment.

"I'm so sorry," I said, somewhat lamely, "But I really don't remember that." And that was the God's honest truth. I have no memory of ever doing such a dastardly thing, and he never told me what led up to the incident. Although no real harm had apparently been done, the accusation haunts me even as I write. I have too much love for others today to think that I hurt someone so long ago. Learning that he has passed away hurts me even more.

Seeing my old classmates, some of whom started with me as early as kindergarten. took me back to my elementary school days. I remembered how I fumbled through a first-grade piano recital. I groaned aloud as I struggled through "Country Gardens," losing my place several times. A classmate, who was My Page Turner, rescued me each time by pointing to my place on the sheet music.

I remember seeing my mother's expression of concern for me as she watched me bow and walk back to my seat. But she could not shield me from the embarrassment I surely felt. However, at the high school reunion, My Page Turner confessed she did not recall that horrible moment so painfully seared into my memory.

I vowed that day I would make my mother proud of me. I believe I kept that promise:

My mother took great pride in my journalism career. And she was extremely proud of my two productions – The Miss Black Teenage Pageant and the Mister African American program. Both programs displayed the talents and positive attributes of area youths, while extolling the virtues of higher education as well as offering educational scholarships.

My earnings as a journalist allowed me to shower my mother with expensive gifts – a silver fox stole, beautiful music boxes, sterling silverware, a scarf from Hermes made in Paris.

A third marriage brought great happiness to my mother. Clinton Williams, a native of Elmira, New York, was a physical therapist at Martland Medical Center in Newark, which later became University Hospital.

Sadly, we lost our dear mother on February 28, 1996. She was 90 years old.

### Ode to my Mother, Nettie E. Williams

*Dearest Mother, I remember when we were young, how the days seemed to drone endlessly on until you came home from work.*

*I remember how it seemed as if fireworks exploded when you walked through the door.*

*I remember how we ran to meet you screaming, "Mommy!" I remember how we vied for your warm hugs. I remember.*

Chapter Four:

# My Marriages

IN 1947, I MARRIED CRAWFORD Daniels, a southerner ten years older than me. A handsome, strapping young man, he grew up on a farm in Johnston, South Carolina with seven siblings and parents, Sally and James. In 1944, the Daniels family quickly left Johnston after young Crawford shot at whites who were harassing him as he walked along a road leading to his home. The family pulled up stakes, leaving a thriving farm to escape the wrath of whites who were sure to react to the young upstart's audacity. The family settled on Walnut Street in Roselle, several blocks from our home on Seventh Avenue.

I met Crawford at Second Baptist Church in Roselle, which both our families attended. The church message was one of hellfire and brimstone, women members shouted their amens, some worked themselves into a frenzy. At Second Baptist, Crawford and I sang in the church choir. Church meetings led to romance and our eventual marriage.

Four beautiful sons, Crawford Solon Daniels, Stephen Douglas Daniels, Bernard James Daniels and Charles Clinton Daniels were born of our marriage.

Meanwhile, my Cousin Gladys married and moved out from my grandmother's home on Eighth Avenue to live in a nearby house on Ninth Avenue in Roselle owned by her new husband, Jimmy

White. She invited me, Crawford Sr. and our first-born, Crawford Solon to live with them. It was a cozy arrangement.

Gladys and Jimmy had no children and smothered our baby son with love and affection. Eventually, I was with child again. After the birth of our second child, Stephen Douglas, Crawford and I decided it was time to strike out on our own.

In mid-1949, we bought a two-story house on Ward Street in Orange, N. J., a little more than nine miles north of Roselle. It was a largely Italian neighborhood. Crawford and I were among the first black families to integrate the neighborhood. There was no welcome mat.

In fact, it was the first – and last – time in my life, I ever experienced being called the "N-word."

I was walking on my way home from a nearby grocery store. That insult came from none other than a young white child standing beside her grinning mother on the second level of a screened-in porch several doors from my new home.

"Did your mother teach you that?" I asked, looking up. "What did you say?" The child's mother demanded in a threatening manner, as if daring me to repeat the question. I knew the woman heard me. I kept walking. I was in no mood for entanglement with her.

Almost immediately after our move there, Crawford and I watched "For Sale" signs spring up. As we settled in on the second floor, the homes around us sold quickly. Although a few white families remained, before we knew it there were black families on either side of us. To supplement our income, we rented the first floor to a black family.

Eventually, two more children were added to our brood, Bernard James on September 28, 1951 and Charles Clinton on June 30, 1953.

About two years after our move to Orange, trouble reared its ugly head in what I thought, at first, was a perfect marriage.

The major source of our problem came in the form of heavy drinking by my husband Crawford and his buddies. Also, I was totally lost when it came to cooking southern favorites – grits, greens, pig's feet, hogshead cheese, chitterlings and the like.

I was unprepared to cope with what I perceived to be the southern male mentality, which surpassed even the sexist mentality of society in general at that time.

In my husband's view, a good wife didn't question her husband's activities or decisions. My "place" was cooking, cleaning, taking care of the children. I had expected more of a partnership, a give and take relationship.

Our differing expectations brought about a lot of friction between us.

Fortunately, my cooking did improve to the point that a dinner guest took a bite out of one of my freshly baked-from-scratch hot-buttered biscuits and began to cry. "This reminds me of my mother," he professed through tears, reaching for a second biscuit.

Meanwhile, the meat packing plant where Crawford worked in Newark was down-sizing. As a result, he was among several employees laid-off. Fortunately, Crawford had a knack for auto repair and was able to use some of our savings to open Daniels Auto Body Shop on Park Street, a block from our home.

While Crawford gained a reputation as the best auto body repairman in the state (a claim voiced by several insurance agents), his drinking escalated and his buddies found the shop a great place to visit, to drink and gamble.

Raised in a family that tolerated neither gambling nor drinking, it was a source of constant bickering between us. It got so bad that if I called the shop to tell Crawford his dinner was ready – and if he lost a hand at cards because of the interruption – he would come home in a violent rage. Our sons, by now the age of concern, would take up positions as if to protect me. It never went further than that, thank God.

The drinking and gambling at the shop came to the attention of the then pastor at Ebenezer Baptist Church, situated diagonally across from the shop on Park Street. He called me to say how troubled he was about the situation. And wives, whose husbands were indulged in the goings-on at the shop, were calling me as well. There was not a thing *I* could do to put a stop to it.

During summer times over the years, we would plan Sunday picnics in nearby Orange Park. I'd cook fried chicken, biscuits, potato salad, green beans and a cake. We'd take off to the park. But Crawford was often somewhere else drinking or gambling – or both.

I was sad for the children who so looked forward to our being together. It really dampened their spirits. We picnicked without him. The boys would be upset, "Where's Dad," they wanted to know. I had no answer. This kind of thing kept me and Crawford quarreling. Unfortunately, there was no Iyanla Van Sant or Dr. Phil to step in.

Still, however, I forged ahead in the marriage, always hoping things would get better.

But my life was about to change. Little did I know how dramatic the change would be for me and the family. The opportunity in sales was just the beginning, an opening up of new opportunities and the development of a sense of confidence I had not displayed or experienced before.

One sunny afternoon a woman named Anna Smith paid me a visit. She was selling, china, crystal and sterling silverware for the now defunct Grace China Co. The china was lovely. I bought an eight- piece set. Not only was the china lovely, but broken pieces were replaced free of charge.

But Anna wasn't satisfied with just making the sale, she wanted to recruit me for the company's sales force.

"You like this too much not to sell it," she said. "I'm too shy for that," I protested. "I could never knock on the doors of strangers."

Yet, Anna saw in me a capability I never imagined I possessed. She persisted, visiting me twice more, trying to convince me to sell Grace China products.

Too timid to give Anna an emphatic "No," I told Crawford, "I'll go with her, watch her make a sale and tell her I hated it. That should settle it."

The reverse happened.

In fact, when I saw Anna make a hefty sale, I asked for a sales kit and lit out on my own. I was so successful and the money was so unbelievably good, I chose to work only two days a week.

*The Force within was stirring!*

Though the pay was excellent, convincing women to fork over a substantial sum for Grace China products had its challenges: I had to be extremely careful of flirtatious husbands who were mostly, of course, picking up the tab.

So, I was always sure to pitch only to the female customer. My biggest sale was an eight-piece set *each* of china, crystal and sterling silverware. My customer loved the products and her husband, an oil delivery man, seemed happy to indulge her. I was on cloud nine. It would be my largest sale during the two years I spent working for the company.

A few days later, however, my customer's husband found his way to my Ward Street home. I was shocked to see him when I answered the door. He was delivering oil a few doors down, he said.

"I thought I'd just stop by to say "Hello.""

I was so flabbergasted I couldn't find words. But Shep, our new German shepherd puppy, took over, growling menacingly, ready to attack. Fortunately, German shepherds grow to a good size very quickly while still puppies and can easily frighten someone off.

"Can't you control that dog?" my uninvited visitor asked. "No," I replied sheepishly. He turned and quickly left, Shep, nipping at his heels.

That day, I found a new appreciation for Shep. Unfortunately, the Grace China Company later claimed bankruptcy and closed its doors.

Meanwhile in the late 1950s and early 1960s, a long simmering tempest of social unrest began to surface in Orange. A big issue – among others – was the gerrymandering of Oakwood Avenue School district, a largely black neighborhood. Area black students were routinely routed to Oakwood, while white students, who lived near there, were bussed to largely white schools in upscale neighborhoods. Another issue was the complete lack of black representation on Orange city council.

I hate to admit it but I was oblivious to this apparent racism in Orange, the place we chose to live out our dreams. Except for such things as Crawford's constant territorial "war" with Italian tow truck owners and the white flight we experienced when we first arrived, I was acutely unaware of the deeper racial issues in Orange.

Education-wise my sons attended schools in our residential district and fared well. I was a regular participant in parent-teacher meetings and was very satisfied with their teachers.

But a new organization, Citizens for Representative Government, (CRG) was being formed to address the issues of gerrymandering and to elect the first black councilman in the history of Orange. The group rallied behind Ernie Thompson, an organizer from Jersey City, which is about 12 miles from Orange. It was Thompson's job to awaken a seemingly sleepy constituency to the power which Orange's black citizenry possessed but which was somehow lying dormant.

In 1962, though not really a joiner, I was somehow compelled to attend a CRG meeting. As I looked around at those gathered there, I realized I didn't know anyone. I began to question myself about why I even came. But I stayed, not wanting to bring attention to myself by getting up to leave.

*My being there was, of course, all God's work.*

The discussion was animated and I must have said something meaningful because I suddenly found myself assigned Chair of the Women's Division to Elect Ben Jones to Council. CRG would also back the mayoral candidate, Nick Franco, a liberal. They would be on the same ticket. If we succeeded in our efforts, Benjamin Jones would make history.

Given such an important task, filled me with pride and a source of energy. I was raring to go, get it done. The women who worked with me were just as eager as I was. We split up the wards we would canvas in our effort to get Ben Jones and Nick Franco elected.

**Jean with first Black Councilmen Ben Jones and Mayor Nick Franco**

Months passed. Election night, 1963, we held our breaths as the votes were tallied. It was disheartening at first. Ben Jones and Nick Franco seemed to be losing until – the votes in the ward where I campaigned for them came in 2-1 for Ben and Nick! Orange had its first black city councilman!

*God's work again!*

I was exuberant. I had actually gone door to door in my ward, stressing the need for black representation on our city council. It resonated. They heard me! They showed up! They voted! We won! We made history! I could feel my confidence soaring as never before.

And just in time. My sons were growing up fast, moving in their own individual lanes.

Crawford, now 16, was showing serious interest in a young lady several doors away. He also talked about starting a community newsletter that would highlight social issues free to the public.

Stephen, 14, had thoughts of starting a band. When he announced these plans, it a came as a total surprise. "Mom. I want to start a band and I need a set of drums." he said with urgency in his voice. He had not spoken or shown any interest in getting a group together before.

"But other than the bass drum, you've never played drums or had lessons," I protested – on the way to the music store.

**Betty and Jean at high school reunion**

When Bernard and Charles weren't playing baseball with friends, they were helping their dad with small chores at the auto shop.

Meanwhile, Stephen busied himself putting together The Dukes and the Duchess, a six-member teen band consisting of his best friend, John Alston, and four other high school buddies. As the band rehearsed Top 20 songs on weekends, the sound of music wafted throughout the neighborhood from the open windows in our living room.

This venture of my second son set in motion a new path for me, management of a band, something I knew nothing about. I had not considered how being a female would impact my journey in the music business. Female band managers were a rarity in the 1960s. I charged ahead oblivious of the fact that most club owners would not take me seriously, at least during a first meeting.

John Alston, a very shy young boy, became a regular and always welcome visitor to our home. He was indeed like a brother to Steve and like a son to me. All of which I took for granted until in his older years, Johnny bared his inner most feelings to me.

"You were like a mother to me," he told me during a phone conversation. I was moved and choked-up to hear this. Because Johnny lived with his mother, I could not have imagined the influence I unknowingly played in his life. But I thank God for the opportunity to have been a blessing to such a wonderful young man.

Later, the band became The Soul Dukes, an all-male group. These young men became popular very quickly in local clubs and at events. During this time, I served as chauffer. Later, to make sure they had transportation to and from engagements, I invested in a van for them, with the understanding I would be compensated in time.

Since I was already acting as a manager, chauffeuring, booking gigs and signing contracts, I thought it was time to make it official. I sat down with them to discuss it. I proposed a 10% management fee and pledged to get union wages for them. My 10% would be over and above what they earned for their shows. This was to be discussed with their parents.

There was agreement all around, until jealousy reared its ugly head.

About two months later, on a Sunday morning, I was awakened by a phone call from a band member's mother. She complained that I was "taking advantage of our children" by charging a management fee.

"How dare you wake me up on a Sunday morning to tell me that," I chided her. "You had no complaints when I was driving them around, staying with them through the nights and seeing them safely home. "If you think I'm taking advantage of your son, you are free to remove him from the band."

After that phone call, I never heard from her again and her son remained a band member for *two* more years.

Another instance of hostility occurred on a night when the van broke down. I called on a band member's father for help because my station wagon couldn't take everyone home.

There was a moment of silence as he considered the situation. Then in a gruff voice he grumbled, "So, big band lady can't get the boys home, eh?" I was caught off guard by the ugly tone of that remark. I just didn't understand why I deserved that attitude. He did, however, show up and, without even a nod to me, drove off with the band members who couldn't fit in my station wagon.

I learned later he was a retired musician. I assumed then, there was a bit of jealousy behind his hostility. I also felt it aggravated him that, of all people, a *woman* had put his son to work earning good union-scale money, $50 an hour for 4-hour gigs!

Meanwhile, Stephen, always watching for work opportunities, became aware of an upcoming concert starring a new group called The Five Stairsteps. This hot group of siblings out of Chicago was burning up the charts with "O-o-h Child," their 1970s hit. The event was slated for Newark, the hub of Northern New Jersey activity.

"Mom, you've gotta' get us on that show." Stephen implored.

As it turned out, the producer of the show, was Hal Jackson, a popular radio disc jockey in New Jersey and New York. I called his radio show in New Jersey and, surprisingly, he agreed the Soul Dukes could have a spot on the show.

I didn't know it then, but the Soul Dukes would be the stars of that night and Jackson would be forever grateful.

**(Please read Chapter Six: Stephen Daniels for more details)**

Meanwhile, my sons were moving on with their lives in different ways and directions in the 1960s: Crawford was working in the accounting division of Newark's Public Service Department. With his newsletter, "Black Oranges," he was becoming more and more of a community activist. It was during this time, I relinquished management of the Soul Dukes so they could grow beyond my limited capacity. Under new management, the band was soon riding a wave of popularity in new areas, performing in Canada, New York, Washington, D. C., the East Coast and Europe; Bernard was working full-time at his dad's shop and Charles was now a full-fledged member of his brother's band.

And Hal Jackson was so impressed with my management of Stephen's band that he and his then wife, Alice offered me the New Jersey franchise of their new enterprise, Hal Jackson's Miss Black Teenage America, a beauty pageant. Of course, I accepted.

Meanwhile, taking on the challenge of producing a teen beauty pageant was one of two life-changing decisions I was to make. The other decision was to file for divorce.

Although, Crawford and I had just recently purchased a lovely new Tudor-style one-family home in Seven Oaks – a more upscale neighborhood in Orange – the quarrels that characterized our marriage continued.

So, after 21 years of watching my hopes and dreams of being happily married slowly dissipate, I took steps to bring it to an end. The white picket was not to be. I filed for and won a divorce.

On February 9, 1968, I became a free woman. It was not exactly a happy time. Crawford moved out of the new home allowing me to stay until I made other arrangements. It felt strange for a bit but I was consumed with thoughts of the challenges ahead. I had my new life as a single woman and my role as producer of a state-wide teen pageant to keep me busy.

As months went by, things seemed to be going as smoothly as possible in spite of the divorce. I had not yet moved out of the new home and my sons were still living there with me. We were looking forward to Bernard's upcoming graduation from Orange High School.

Finally, that day arrived. June 15, 1969, was a day of happiness for Bernard and our family. Together, we watched him receive his high school diploma. The entire family was thrilled. Afterwards, Bernard left us to attend several graduation parties.

I could never have imagined that, before the night was over, Bernard's happiness would have been short-lived, that he would suffer a horrific injustice at the hands of those he was raised to believe were our protectors.

**(Please read more details in Chapter Six: Bernard Daniels)**

By now, the Soul Dukes were doing marvelously well. At one gig, the band came to the attention of George Hudson, a well-known impresario in the entertainment world. Hudson was so impressed that the young men were not only great musicians but they were also very disciplined.

Hudson approached Stephen with only one question: "Who is your manager?" When Stephen answered, "My mother," Hudson was even more impressed.

He handed Stephen a card, saying, "Tell her to call me in the morning. I need a manager for my new office."

That next morning, I called Hudson, "Anybody who can manage a large male band without being on hand can manage anything, "he said. "I've just opened a radio advertising agency and would like you to work for me."

*God is working here!*

**Newark Sunday News**
August 10, 1969

ON THE AIR — George Hudson and Mrs. Jean Bryant, his associate, set up equipment to record a radio commercial in George Hudson Associates advertising agency studio at 671 Broad St. He is former radio broadcaster.

# Negro Seeks 'Breakthrough' In Advertising Business

**BY HARVEY EKENSTIERNA**
Newark News Financial Writer

George Hudson is a man with a dream of success in the business he started recently in Newark.

He is optimistic about his chances for success despite the tough competition and the color of his skin. He is a Negro who is attempting to break what he terms "the white barrier" into the advertising business.

Hudson was in radio broadcasting for more than 20 years before opening George Hudson Associates in May at 671 Broad St.

A native of Kathleen, Ga., Hudson, 49, was raised in Trenton and studied civil engineering for two years at Purdue University before deciding he belonged in a field more in touch with people.

His activities in singing, acting and radio work at the school led him to a course at Columbia University in radio broadcasting, and he got his first radio job in 1947 on station WTTM in Trenton.

**An Announcer**

He later became a full time staff announcer with WCAP in Asbury Park, which later became WJLK, and in 1953 was the first announcer hired by WNJR in Newark, which was aimed directly at a Black audience.

Although he just opened his counts his advertising and copywriting experience as starting in 1948, when he began writing advertisements, mailing pieces and radio commercials for shows he produced.

His production credits are numerous, including concerts, stage shows and Gospel presentations in Asbury Park's Convention Hall, the old Laurel Garden and Symphony Hall in Newark, at Carnegie Hall in New York, Harlem's Apollo Theatre and several years ago at the New York World's Fair, where he staged a series of Gospel concerts in the New Jersey Pavillion.

**Slowth Growth**

Hudson's start in the advertising business in Newark is presently based completely on Black advertisers shooting for a market of Negro consumers.

Since leaving WNJR in May, his list of clients has been growing slowly, and he claims "moderate success" to date.

He has been workng hard, however, to nail down one big white client. He feels once he has made that breakthrough, other accounts will follow.

Hudson's outlook is realistic. He knows that any new advertising business would have trouble breaking in on the accounts of established agencies, but he feels he has the tools to reach the Black people of the state as no white advertising agency can.

He cites as an example, the efforts of a major wine company, which some time ago flooded Negro areas with an ad which started, "Hey Cats, Dig this. . . "

"We just don't talk like that," Hudson exclaimed, "that ad just missed the mark, and the advertisers are not getting their money's worth. They are being led down the wrong path."

**Missing People**

He added, "White advertising agencies don't know the ghetto, and they are missing hundreds of thousands of people." He firmly believes he can give an advertiser "a lot more mileage" for his dollar, and says "some day some business will step forward and discover a brilliant business step by finding out that a Black agency can sell more."

Hudson is making his pitch to run a recruitment campaign for N.J. Bell Telephone Co., and also has a presentation before Public Service Electric and Gas Co. He has also submitted a program to develop popular support for the Jersey Jays, Newark's professional football entry in the Continental Football League.

He is also developing the format for a television program featuring talented Garden State residents which he hopes to sell on a cooperative basis to all of the state's utility companies to sponsor.

Hudson lives in Montclair with his wife, Ruth, a speech therapist in the East Orange schools, and two daughters, Carole Ann, an art student at Hampton Institute, and Barbara, who works in his office as a file clerk. The Hudsons also have a married daughter, Mrs. Michelle Glover, also of Montclair.

Hudson's optimism is evident from the one-year lease he has taken on the office and sound studio he occupies on the fifth floor of the Wiss Building.

He fully anticipates having to move to larger quarters by the end of the year; expand from his current two employes to eight, and pass the $1 million billing mark.

By his own estimates, a successful Negro advertising agency is one which hits $1.5 million a year in billings, but he has his sights set on $5 million, and after that, he will "break the barrier into television advertising."

I was pleased with the offer to work for what was New Jersey's first black advertising agency. I agreed to meet with him the next day at his new offices in Downtown Newark.

"Wow!" I thought. "This can't be real!" I couldn't wait to meet this man.

George Hudson Associates was located in a sky scraper that rose high above the city of Newark. It was complete with new recording equipment ready to spin ads for radio. And he greeted me warmly. He explained my duties would be light, taking phone calls, placing radio ads, making sure things ran smoothly. I started work the next day.

The job proved perfect for me, for my creative juices. Not only did I place ads with agencies, I wrote the ad copy as well. I found I was quite the idea-person. When the former Newark City Hospital wanted to launch an ad campaign to fight the myriad of social ills then plaguing the city, I designed an advertising campaign for them and put a $10,000 price tag on it. The hospital bought it.

*Thank you, God*

How to keep most of that money in the coffers of George Hudson Associates became the question for us. It was the late 1960s. At the time, Newark was Number One in New Jersey in black infant deaths, in drug abuse and in alcoholism. The hospital had clinics serving people with those problems and desperately wanted the public notified.

I proposed to Hudson that we hire ten media students from local colleges, pay them $100 each to study what each clinic offered. Then we would let the students write copy for the ads. About $9,000 thousand dollars would be kept for the agency.

Hudson loved the idea. And the colleges we contacted were eager to have their students participate, to get hands-on experience.

The response to the resulting ads was so great the hospital reported six new phone lines had to be installed to handle calls.

"I'm going to start tip toeing around you so as not to disturb your brain waves," Hudson said to me, amazed at how well the idea paid off.

Sadly, almost a year later, Hudson suddenly became ill, was hospitalized and died shortly after. I was never advised as to his cause of death. Nonetheless, I kept the office running until the Hudson family could make decisions regarding the future of the business.

Meanwhile, I began to question myself. If asked, could I really take on the responsibility of running George Hudson's business, his dream, something he envisioned would become an important institution in the black community? If somehow the business failed under my leadership, how could I face anyone? I couldn't.

On a particular day, with those thoughts creating havoc with my mind, I took a deep breath and gave notice. Though I was asked to stay on, I remained resolute.

*Well, God, where do I go from here?*

Since it was still early that day, I decided to pay a visit to the New Jersey Afro-American Newspaper to see if they might be hiring. On the outskirts of Newark, its offices were only a short distance away from Hudson Associates.

Part of the Afro-American Newspaper chain headquartered in Baltimore, Maryland, the New Jersey edition was the longest running and most widely read black newspaper in the state.

I didn't know it then, but visiting its Newark office was one of the best decisions I was to ever make, a decision that would lead to my 29-year career as a journalist.

The office was in a somewhat run-down building that stood alone. Much smaller than I expected, the office was headed by Bob Queen, a short, wiry pipe-smoking man who wore suspenders and looked every bit like a news editor.

Seated behind the lobby's reception desk, Queen buzzed me in through the heavy glass door. He remained seated, puffing on his pipe as I introduced myself.

Although we had never met, we knew of each other because his newspaper placed advertisement through George Hudson Associates. In one corner of the lobby, was a stack of the week's newspapers for public consumption.

Queen studied me carefully as he continued to puff on his pipe. "How can I help you?" he asked nonchalantly.

I told him of my decision to leave George Hudson Associates and asked if there were openings at his newspaper in either the advertising or news departments.

"As far as the news is concerned, it's a one-man operation here – editor, photographer and reporter. And I'm it!" Queen said emphatically, quickly adding, "We do need someone in our accounting department. If you're interested, our accounts manager will be leaving soon."

Of course, I was interested! I filled out the required papers. Queen showed me around the small office and introduced me to his equally small staff. The two women who made up the rest of the office personnel headed the advertising and accounting departments. Both delightful women were eager to show me the ropes.

I'll take the job," I told Queen.

"If you like, you can start today." Queen told me.

*Hired on the spot again! God continues to show up for me!*

As it turned out, the job was pretty easy and pretty routine: record money, bank money, pay bills, occasionally take calls. Like George Hudson, Bob Queen proved to be an easy-going boss. He was not as effusive as George but was wonderfully appreciative of my work. However, he continually ignored my hints about hiring me as a news reporter.

My one concern was the neighborhood in which the office was located. It was not very safe at all. I was instructed to keep the office door locked at all times, especially when alone. I understood why when one day, while on my way to deposit the day's receipts at a local bank, I witnessed a group of kids – I guessed to be between eight and 10 years old – surround an elderly woman carrying packages. They pinned her arms to her body, grabbed her packages and quickly disappeared. Those kids were so precise, I was sure an adult was lurking somewhere in a get-a-way car.

Meanwhile, as fate would have it, the opportunity to write literally fell into my lap. It happened on a particular day when I was alone in the office.

Because everyone else had gone to lunch, I had taken a seat at the front desk to answer phones. As I sat alone, I was mindful of instructions from Queen not to answer the door to strangers.

Still, I took a chance when a policeman came to the office door. He was in full uniform, his badge easily seen and his gun was in its holster.

"I have information about a program our precinct is starting for kids in the neighborhood," he said through the glass door. He held up a large folder for me to see. I buzzed him in.

The officer was excited about a program designed to cultivate a relationship with area youths to, hopefully, turn them away from criminal activities. I took notes. When the officer left, I turned to the old typewriter on the lobby desk and fashioned a story.

RY 25, 1971 — 2nd Class Postage Paid at Orange, N. J. 07050 — $7.00 A YEAR By Mail — 20c A Copy

TO AID AND ASSIST is purpose of new advisory committee to Police Community Relations Bureau. From left, front row are Miss A. Lorraine Jones, Mrs. Jean Bryant, Miss Bessie Hunt and Mrs. Pearl Overby. Standing, Det. William Andrews, Dr. Benjamin Shackelford, Lt. Joseph DeAngelis, Chief Eugene Uricoli, Commissioner John Trezza, Eugene Lund and Frank Scura, committee chairman.

# Advisory Committee To Aid Police Bureau

A committee to aid and assist the police in the handling of such problems as juvenile delinquency, alleged police brutalities and narcotics has been formed in Orange.

Frank Scura of 523 Park avenue was named chairman of the Police - Community Relations Advisory Committee to the Police-Community Relations Bureau at a meeting last week. Commissioner John Trezza, public safety director, appointed Scura.

Meetings of the committee will be held on a monthly basis but will be held more frequently if needed.

Many problems have beset the Police Department in recent years, among them and most disruptive have been charges with racial overtones. The committee hopes to offset rumors and get down to facts on both sides of each case and if necessary, refer it to the proper authorities.

"We'll try to let the Commissioners know just where the citizens want to go," said Scura.

"We want the man in the street, the people with children or somebody who has a stake in Orange," he said.

"If we accomplish only one-tenth of what we try to do, that will at least be one-tenth, that wouldn't have been done," said Scura. The chairman said he was available 24 hours a day "to Director Trezza and Chief Eugene Uricoli."

Lt. Joseph DeAngelis is co-ordinator for the Police Community Relations Bureau and Det. William Andrews is a member.

Members of the Advisory

The committee is made up of persons from all walks of life.

"Problems would be sent to our committee and we would talk about it," explained Scura, adding, "a lot of voices are better than one voice."

He said he had "sat back" long enough and now wants to help.

"It's easy to run away," Scura philosophized, "but no matter how far west you go you'll always come back to the east because the globe is round."

The chairman said he would like three or four representatives from each ward and from all walks of life on the commit-

(Continued on Page 6)

**Jean on Orange Police Advisory Board**

*The Inner Force – God -- was working again. Other than my attempt as an eight-year-old, I had not written a story since. But some-*

*thing compelled me to turn to that old typewriter and take on the challenge.*

"He'll either be pleased or annoyed." I thought.

On Queen's return to the office, I told him what I had done. Looking for a sign of approval, I handed him the finished script, which he took a minute to peruse. Was Queen pleased? I couldn't tell. He said nothing. He nodded his head and retreated silently to his office. I could only think the story wasn't good enough for print.

I decided to put it out of my mind and went about my duties in accounting, which now was my sole responsibility.

A week passed. Once again, I was seated at the front desk on a weekday morning. I was alone drinking coffee, when I buzzed in our circulation manager. Loaded down with new editions of the newspaper, he left a stack in the usual corner for the public, then left to continue his deliveries.

Queen soon arrived. He said his usual "Good morning," pulled two copies of the newspaper from the stack, placed one copy on my desk and disappeared into his office. I took a sip of coffee, reached for the paper. And there it was – my story on Page One! A headline. A byline! I raced breathlessly into Queen's office.

"Bob! You put my story on Page One!"

Queen sat calmly, knowingly prepared for my outburst. He planned it! He knew it was coming! A sly smile crossed his face as he lit his pipe and leaned back in his chair, while I thanked him profusely.

Back in my office, a moment of self-doubt over took me. Could I really write stories on a consistent basis? Could I meet deadlines?

*I didn't ponder long. My confidence was quickly restored -- God again! I went back to my office overjoyed.*

Thus, began my 29-year career as a journalist.

Queen told me later, that he had never considered me for the reporter's job because over the years so many people had come through the door professing the ability to write. And, they always failed. He had become resigned to doing the job himself.

*That innate force that imbued me with desire to express myself through writing when I was eight years old, had finally come of age and would no longer be denied. Undeniably God's work!*

I spent two glorious years working for the Afro-American newspaper before leaving New Jersey to join my new husband, Dewey Bryant, in Pittsburgh.

Meanwhile, Stephen's band once again came to the attention of a famed personality. When The Five Stairsteps, the hottest new band in the country, got stuck in Chicago and failed to appear at the scheduled concert, the *unscheduled* Soul Dukes took the stage. They played most of the Stairsteps' album, thus, saving the day for Promoter Hal Jackson, one of the best-known radio disc jockeys on the East Coast.

That encounter between the Soul Dukes and Hal Jackson became fruitful for both me and Stephen. A grateful Jackson sent gigs the band's way and Jackson and his then wife, Alice, offered me the New Jersey franchise in their new venture, Hal Jackson's Miss Black Teenage America beauty pageant.

*Thank you, God*

The franchise didn't come with many instructions and I knew nothing about putting on a beauty pageant – except what I had seen watching Miss America. To get a better idea of what might be expected at such an event, I looked up the word *pageant* in Webster's Dictionary. The words *spectacle, splendor, parade,* caught my attention.

With those words in mind, my plans unfolded and were shared with a small staff of volunteers, amassed from responses to my newspaper ads for help. These volunteers assisted me in helping the young ladies learn stage presence, choose proper gowns and refine their talents.

Among the volunteers was Charles Howe, Editorial Assistant in the Publications Division of Prudential Insurance Co. in Newark. His expertise was vital in helping me navigate media.

With his help, I secured servicemen from the Army, Navy and Marines, as escorts for our contestants, who ranged in age from 13 to 17 years old. About 10 young men from local college ROTC groups responded to our calls, several white servicemen among them. Each serviceman would extend an arm to a young lady and guide her onto the stage. The servicemen would rotate until each young lady had been escorted. the Soul Dukes would play appropriate background music for the presentation of contestants and entertain during breaks.

But not everyone shared my vision.

On Saturday, June 26, 1971, the eve of the event, everything seemed to be going well – at first. Excitement filled the air at The Terrace Ball Room in Newark, where the event would take place. Contestants, volunteers and the armed services had shown up in full force for a last rehearsal.

Just before I dismissed everyone, I decided to take a bathroom break. I was still in a stall when in walked two volunteers, who helped train contestants. Neither had any idea I was in there. The conversation went like this:

"Ugh," said one, "this is awful. It's too much like a wedding. I really don't want to be a part of this." The other volunteer expressed similar feelings. "I don't like this either," she said. "It's almost laughable."

I was stunned, shocked at what I heard. When I stepped out of the stall, My Two Back Stabbers stood petrified, not knowing what to expect from me. I washed my hands and left the bathroom, without even a glance toward them, saying nothing.

When rehearsal finally ended, I chose not to let anyone know of the incident and bravely gave everyone last minute instructions. I did not let on how crushed I really was.

I went home, where my new husband, Dewey Bryant awaited me. He had flown in from Pittsburgh as he often did since our marriage. Distraught at the criticism I'd heard from My Two Back Stabbers, I was almost hysterical. My tears were flowing.

"They said it's going to be a horrible show," I sobbed. "I don't think my volunteers are going to show up."

Stop crying," Dewey pleaded. "*You can* do this. Just get some paper and write down how *you* want the show to go."

A script! Why hadn't I thought of that? I sat at my trusty typewriter, fingers flying over the keys as Dewey egged me on for several pages.

I felt better now. Instead of notes, my show was scripted. The backstage crew, Stephen and certain trusted volunteers would get copies. The main folks would know *what* was happening and *when* it would be happening. On cue, contestants would appear.

Sunday, June 27 1971. Showtime!

I arrived at the Terrace Ballroom somewhat apprehensive, scripts in hand. I entered the ballroom and was aghast! The place was packed, filled to capacity! All volunteers – including My Two Back Stabbers – were there. The Armed Services looked splendid in dress uniforms. I gave out the scripts, took a deep breath, straightened my shoulders and forged ahead.

*That Force – God – was right on time, moving me, pressing me forward with a renewed vigor.*

I took a quick check, stood at my newly scripted place at the end of the runway stage and gave the signal to start the show.

The Soul Dukes began playing the Joe Cocker hit, "You are so Beautiful" as contestants, in a beautiful array of colors, appeared slowly from behind stage in their gowns. The Army, Navy, and Marine volunteers stepped forward as each contestant approached and escorted the thrilled young ladies to the stage. The audience clapped, shouted, whistled approval!

My Two Back Stabbers soon realized there was a new sheriff in town. They meekly took seats in the audience and stayed out of my way.

Hal Jackson dropped in to check us out. He was amazed at the size of our crowd. He whispered to me that two nationally known recording stars were appearing in a nearly empty theater next door to the Terrace.

"*This* is where they should have been," he laughed.

At the end of the competition, 15-year-old Anita Jo Bracey of Oakhurst, Monmouth County, about 45 miles from Newark, was crowned. I was beset with congratulatory hugs from contestants, parents and patrons.

It was a night to remember: a lovely teenager wore a sparkling crown, she was queen of them all, and she was being hailed by her community, all of whom adored her.

"You don't know what you did for Black people tonight!" One woman exclaimed to me as she was leaving the show.

At home that night, however, things took on a more serious turn.

Dewey wanted to talk about our marriage, which had largely consisted of him making weekend flights to see me. It had been a year since we married in a small ceremony at my mother's home in Roselle. I still had not made the move to Pittsburgh, Dewey's home town.

A Pittsburgh narcotics detective, Dewey and I met in a night club in Newark. He and another detective were in the city to attend a police convention. My good friend, Pat Clemente and I were at the club for a girls' night out.

As the music played that night, Dewey's eyes locked with mine. He approached me and asked me to dance. I was somewhat hesitant. I'd been divorced about a year and still felt rather shy about meeting other men. However, before I knew it, I was on my feet and in Dewey's arms slow dancing to "Little Green Apples." Pat wasn't doing too badly either. She was smiling a lot and seemed to be having fun with Dewey's buddy. After we left the club, Dewey and I kept in touch, eventually falling in love and marrying.

Now, this night – while I was still riding high from the success of the pageant – Dewey wanted to discuss our future.

"I feel guilty asking you to leave all this," he said. "But we can't go on living apart."

Of course, I knew we could not live separately forever and maintain a healthy marriage. At the same time, I was reluctant to leave Orange and my children. I just couldn't seem to set a date for moving to Pittsburgh. Leaving my children and family was the hardest decision of my life. I told Dewey I needed more time. He agreed.

Later, I sat down with my sons, who were already carving out their own lives.

Stephen, 24, had new management for the Soul Dukes and was about to spend a month at a club in Mexico City, Mexico; Charles, now 20 and a full-fledged member of Soul Dukes Band, would be with Stephen in Mexico; Bernard, 22, was now working full-time for his father at Daniels Auto Body Shop and Crawford, 26, had a full-time job at Public Service in Newark and had already fathered his first child, a daughter, Toni.

In a group conversation with all four sons, there were no objections to my decision to move to Pittsburgh. It was established their dad would keep close tabs on them in the new home in Seven Oaks, while I would be making frequent visits.

"I will only be a telephone call away." I promised.

Meanwhile, the pressure was on not only for me to join my husband, Dewey, in Pittsburgh, but to also set a date for the 2nd annual Miss Black Teenage New Jersey pageant before I left for the Smokey City. Added to that, Hal and Alice Jackson offered me the franchise for a Miss Black Teenage pageant in Pittsburgh. Of course, I accepted!

*What in the world was I thinking? Two pageants in different states? It seemed I really wasn't thinking. But a Force – it had to be God – was guiding me, supporting me.*

Before heading for Steeler Country, I set June 25th 1972 as the date for the second New Jersey event. I rounded up an entirely new and trusted committee, which included Johnny Alston, Stephen's best friend since their teen years, and longtime family friend, Sandra Hughes. The new committee would execute the same exact plans as the first show. I would return to New Jersey in time to pull it all together.

It was early January 1972 when I landed at Pittsburgh International Airport. Dewey was there to greet me. The sky was cloudy, grey as it had been on my first visit made shortly before we married. I wondered: "Does the sun *ever* shine in Pittsburgh?

My new life in Pittsburgh proved to be a big adjustment. I had always lived on tree-lined streets. I grew up in houses with front lawns, a back yard. Row houses were unfamiliar to me.

Now, here I was in my new home, a row house on Beldale Street, in Pittsburgh's North Side neighborhood. Soon after my arrival, Dewey introduced me to neighbors, family, and his friends. Over time, I liked them all. North Siders, I determined, were good, decent, down-to-earth folks.

Dewey's three sons, Thomas (Tommy), Kenneth ("Juice") and Richard ("Kip") Bryant, were polite youngsters who I came to love as my own. They lived with their mother, Martha and her second husband, Milton Ward. A daughter, Sue, was born of that union.

Once I was settled, Dewey, knowing my desire to continue writing, suggested the names of the two newspapers he thought I would want an interview with namely, the Pittsburgh Press, a major daily, and the New Pittsburgh Courier, a black weekly. I called both newspapers but the Pittsburgh Press, located on the Boulevard of the Allies, Downtown, responded first.

My interview with Pittsburgh Press Executive Editor Leo Koeberlein, now deceased, went extremely well. I submitted a portfolio of stories I'd written for the New Jersey Afro-American. He read them quickly before expressing a major concern. "Your background is with a weekly newspaper. Do you think you can handle a daily news deadline?"

I didn't think twice, before answering, "Yes."

I was hired on the spot, thereby becoming the first African-American female reporter hired in the history of the Pittsburgh Press, then the largest newspaper in Western Pennsylvania.

*God is working again!*

Koeberlein, indicated he expected me to start working immediately and was amused when I begged off for time to acquire a wardrobe that would accommodate a daily schedule. A quick shopping spree took care of that situation. A few days later, I was on the payroll.

A favorite early memory of mine is walking past an alley one morning on my way to a bus stop to get to my new job. That morning, a television show aired regarding my plans to bring Hal Jackson's Miss Black Teenage America pageant to Pittsburgh. As I looked toward the alley, there stood a man so inebriated he had to hold onto the edge of a house.

Our eyes met. "I j-just saw y-you on TV," the man stammered. I chuckled to myself, nodded and smiled in his direction. "I hope the show didn't drive him to drink," I joked to myself.

I really loved my job at the Press. Editors usually handed out assignments for news or feature stories to reporters. Sometimes, readers contacted us with story ideas. Or I would submit my own story ideas to editors.

Often, I wrote stories that were not only informative but were, in some instances, life-changing. One of my favorite stories involved a bank employee who had been arrested for a robbery he did not commit. Although another man with an almost identical profile who lived in another state confessed to the crime, the local bank had never restored the status of its innocent employee. That all changed after I wrote of his dilemma.

In another story, a Westmoreland County man reported his wife missing. The "color" in my story led to the woman's body. I wrote: "Her husband drove a *black Cadillac*. She drove a *pink Cadillac*." An observant reader called police to say he had seen a *black* Cadillac parked in a wooded area near a veterans' club. Police investigated and found the woman's body buried there. Her husband was arrested and charged with her murder.

Another one of my favorite stories was about Donny Merlo, 17 of Carrick., a Pittsburgh suburb. On Oct. 28, 1979, Donny bravely stepped out on the playing field to join his high school band. It was Carrick Community Day. What the crowd didn't realize was that Donny, the student field conductor, had just been diagnosed with cancer and the outlook was grim. Donny wanted no one to know about his upcoming battle. He gamely carried out his responsibilities.

I never knew the final outcome of Donny's surgery. But some ten years later, a very handsome young man with a thick mane of black hair, stopped me in Downtown Pittsburgh. "Are you Jean Bryant," he asked. Curiously, I answered "yes."

"I'm Donny Merlo!"

His pronouncement took my breath away! I was so elated. The young man who had so bravely stepped out on that high school field so many years ago facing, perhaps the biggest challenge of his life, had won his battle! He was alive and well!

Over the years such stories kept me busy and editors seemed satisfied with my work.

The Press, like many newspapers in that era, was undergoing demographic changes. Soon after I was hired, more women and black writers were joining the reporting staff and improving coverage of the black community.

I kept my commitment to presenting a second New Jersey Miss Black Teenage event. John Alston and Sandra Hughes pulled it off beautifully and there was little for me to do. Another Fabulous show, another beautiful queen and a grateful community.

Back home in Pittsburgh, it seemed I hardly had time to breathe before it was time to begin placing ads in newspapers to solicit contestants and volunteers for the first Miss Black Teenage America Pittsburgh Finals. The date was set for May 13, 1973, Mothers' Day.

And it wasn't long before discouraging comments were getting back to me: "No one would attend a pageant on such a sacred day." And "Pittsburgh is just a shot-and–a-beer town. A pageant wouldn't be of much interest here."

However, I learned my lesson in New Jersey. Don't listen to naysayers. I stayed on course. I Placed ads about the upcoming event and waited. The resulting responses from eager pageant applicants and from volunteers who just wanted to be of help, filled me with encouragement and buoyed my hopes.

*Thank you, God.*

Finally, in late March, rehearsals for Hal Jackson's Miss Black Teenage America Pittsburgh finals began. There was excitement all around as contestants, parents, me and my volunteer committee met in the offices of WAMO Radio, then located Uptown on the Boulevard of the Allies. The late Bill Powell, then director of Public Relations for the station, was instrumental in obtaining our usage of its small theater, where we rehearsed free of charge.

Plans for this first-time event progressed nicely: The Soul Dukes would make their first Pittsburgh appearance at the show; pageant preliminaries and the pageant finals were set for Soldiers and Sailors Memorial Hall in Pittsburgh's Oakland section. An array of

Pittsburgh's elite was chosen as preliminary and finals judges for the show. And rehearsals with our 59 contestants were going well.

I was ecstatic. But my bubble was burst when, at a conference with parents, I was met with sarcasm from one mother.

"You come to Pittsburgh doing this, when some of us already here had it in mind to do," she said with acrimony. "We really don't know you or who you really are!"

Her words shocked me. She made it sound like I had undermined *her* plans. I wasn't sure how to respond. Then, another mother spoke up, completely shutting down this attack against me.

*God shows up when the enemy attacks.*

"I am very satisfied with what this program has done for *my* daughter and I think most of us feel the same way I do," the other mother said emphatically. She was joined by several others who chimed in with similar comments. Nothing further was said by the disgruntled woman. I chalked it up to jealousy of some sort. Things went smoothly after that.

On Mothers' Day, the first annual Miss Black Teenage America Pittsburgh finals went off without a hitch. The New Pittsburgh Courier gave us splendid coverage. The pageant drew a crowd of about 1,000 people. Renee Moore, a beautiful 15-year-old teenager from Wilkinsburg, a Pittsburgh suburb, was crowned the first Pittsburgh queen. Her parents, Gwen and George Moore, both now deceased, became loyal volunteers and were helpful in many ways as the pageant grew in importance to the community.

Early, the next day after the pageant, the phone rang and I answered.

"Hello, Jean. I see you had a very successful show last night. Congratulations!" the male voice said. "I'm an old friend of Dewey's. Let me speak to him, please."

Dewey took the phone, listened to his "old friend" and told him, "Hold on a minute. Let me talk to my wife."

Seems the "old friend" needed $3,000. He was behind on his mortgage and asked Dewey if we could spot him for a loan ASAP. "Can we help him out?" Dewey asked me. It upset me that Dewey even considered it and I shook my head "no."

As time went on, I began to realize that Dewey was behind in several bills. I pretended not to notice this predicament and offered to take on two responsibilities – buying the food and paying the phone bills. This pleased Dewey to some extent. "I really don't use the phone that much," he said.

Then, during a trip to his favorite butcher on the North Side's Woods Run area, Dewey casually ordered enough T- bone steaks to feed an army.

"Cut 'em thick, Joe!" he ordered.

"Well, that's what freezers are for," I thought.

Our need to know each other better became apparent when Dewey called me from work one day. His crew had busted a drug ring. They were confiscating stolen goods.

"There are some beautiful clothes if you want anything, Darling," he informed me.

"No, Dewey, I don't *ever* want anything like that!" I said emphatically. "I *never* want anything to do with stolen goods!" He told me later, that he was glad I had refused.

That was just one incident that revealed our different mindsets. Another occurred one evening when Dewey and I were attending a dinner party at a local restaurant with a group of his detective friends. We were about to enter the facility, when a tall, thin young man – seemly in his early 20s – approached the couple in front of us with what turned out to be a stolen diamond ring.

The young man had no way of knowing this was a group of plain-clothesmen dressed for a night out. I was stunned when the detective who the kid approached grabbed the kid, pushed him up against a wall of the building, took the ring from him, put it on his wife's finger and told the kid to "scram!" His wife's face was flushed with embarrassment. She sat in quiet discomfort the entire evening, not daring to take off the ring and hardly touching her food.

There seemed to be some discomfort amongst the group of detectives but no one took it upon themselves to reproach their buddy about his action.

And I wondered what that kid thought when he saw what happened to the ring.

My concerns about my relationship with Dewey continued, but for the next few months, everything in life was feeling cozy. I was in love, I felt loved, I loved my job at the Pittsburgh Press and my colleagues were warm and friendly.

Meanwhile, the third annual Miss Black Teenage New Jersey finals was a success. On June 17, 1973, the show went on without a hitch. When I arrived in New Jersey, there was little for me to do. The new committee followed my scripts and handled things beautifully. Once again, the Terrace Ballroom Room was packed. Once again, the night was magical.

I returned to Pittsburgh feeling on top of the world. Not only that, my husband was now taking me to work mornings and picking me up evenings. And he had dinner warmed and waiting for me, all this before he left for his night shift at work.

"Boy are you lucky," noted a colleague, "You're getting door-to-door service." And yes, it felt good – coming home to the smell of garlic, onions, and steak permeating throughout the house. What could be better than this?

It was about this time, I got bad news from Mexico City, where the Soul Dukes were engaged. Son Stephen called to tell me his brother Charles had been arrested during a drug raid on the club where they were appearing. He was taken to Lecumberri, a prison with a notorious reputation for corruption and torture of prisoners.

**(Please read Chapter Six: Charles Daniels for more details)**

Meanwhile, with a heavy heart at Charles' imprisonment, I began working to keep my commitment with the Jacksons to produce the New Jersey and Pittsburgh Miss Black Teenage America pageants again. Once again, I secured the Terrace Ballroom in New Jersey and Soldiers and Sailors Memorial Hall in Pittsburgh.

Each pageant was a demanding project. Work for the next year's pageant would begin almost immediately after the current year's finals.

My taking on the production of two pageants soon became irritating to Dewey. The constant "crises" phone calls from committee members – often during hours when Dewey and I were trying to relax – were mostly regarding minor problems with contestants or parents.

I even got an urgent call from the leader of a group producing a Hal Jackson pageant in a nearby state. It seems they heard my radio ads in Pittsburgh and wanted my advice regarding their organizational problems.

"It got so bad at one of our meetings a gentleman threw a chair across the room," the caller said. I was invited to their next meeting.

Dewey advised me to not to accept the invitation and I whole heartedly agreed with him. I surmised that the group called me instead of Hal Jackson because they feared losing the franchise if the Jacksons learned of their disarray. After I declined, I heard no more from that group. However, their state wound up entering a contestant in the nationals, which led me to deduce the issues had been resolved.

Producing two pageants was not only creating problems in my marriage, but was also wearing me down. I thought it best to give up the New Jersey finals. I decided not to proceed with those plans another year. The 1973 pageant would be the last for New Jersey.

However, the decision saddened me. After all, the New Jersey venture had maintained its popularity, it was a blessing to the teens that participated, it provided me a chance to visit family in New Jersey and it provided work for Stephen and his band.

Also, sometime later, Hal and Alice made a fundamental change in the Miss Black Teenage America pageant. They gave it a new name: Hal Jackson's U. S. Talented Teens Pageant. The word "black" would no longer to be used.

Alice explained that she and Hal believed it was time to integrate their pageant. They believed they could attract more funding from diverse resources as an integrated entity instead of relying on "blackness" to attract corporate interests.

They had no objections to my continuing the Miss Black Teenage America pageant as my own enterprise in Pittsburgh and released me from contract. I renamed my pageant simply, Miss Black Teenage, no regional limitations. However, the Jacksons asked me to produce their newest venture – Miss U. S. Talented Teen – in Pittsburgh. And I agreed.

Meanwhile, I rejoiced at the thought of turning the Miss Black Teenage Pageant into my very own creation, with my unique ideas. One of my first moves was to invent a pageant motto, "Confidence, Awareness and Pride" (CAP), values we hoped to instill in each young lady. We emphasized that wearing this "CAP" at all times would be instrumental in the success of all their endeavors.

Another idea was to show support for young black males. I decided to choose a black male college student and support him with a $500 yearly stipend over four years of college. Our first – and last – recipient was Hart Coleman, a Carnegie Mellon University student.

As a graduating senior, Hart wrote me: "With the assistance of the Miss Black Teenage Pageant, I have achieved a quality education at Carnegie Mellon University. I want to express my deepest gratitude to Mrs. Bryant and her staff for their kindness over the past four years."

Finding and tracking a recipient for the grant involved a bit more work than I had anticipated. Regretfully, I dropped the idea from the Miss Black Teenage program.

I continued the Miss Black Teenage pageant in Pittsburgh for the next 29 years, opening it up to more Pennsylvania counties, tailoring it to reflect my specific ideas, my way of thinking. During rehearsals with the young ladies, I put more emphasis on education, providing more educational (cash) scholarships, and exposing contestants to positive role models.

Rehearsals were scheduled 9:00 a.m. to 5:00 p.m. eight Saturdays in a row, two absences meant dismissal from the pageant. Singing, dancing and acting coaches were added to bring each contestant up to her greatest potential; guest speakers were brought in to discuss the ills of drugs, bullying and other teen issues.

I'm not sure if changing the name of the Jackson's pageant attracted more diverse contestants for them but my first Miss U.S. Talented Teens pageant in 1974 fared pretty well in that regard. Half of our 25 contestants were white. I found resistance, however, from some committee members about the idea of an integrated pageant.

"You are just providing one more opportunity for white girls," was a common argument. I'm happy to say that once we agreed it was going to happen, everyone came aboard.

I chose Webster Hall in the Oakland section of Pittsburgh as the venue for this first Miss U.S. Talented Teens Pageant. Since the number of contestants was so much smaller than the number of contestants in Miss Black Teenage pageants, Webster Hall was the better choice. Also, contestants stayed in rooms at the hall, which is now used as apartment dormitories for Carnegie Mellon University students.

Meanwhile, the second year (1975), a larger number of contestants participated in the U. S. Talented Teen pageant and again, a goodly number were white. It was during our last Talented Teens rehearsal when I noticed a young woman I had not seen before just casually walking around. She was not one of the contestants and I did not recognize her at all. But I reasoned to myself that she was probably a relative of one of the contestants. So, I didn't question her or keep a watch over her.

Big mistake!

At the end of rehearsal, contestants went back stage to retrieve their belongings and found things in disarray. They had been robbed! I believed I knew who had done it. It had to have been that strange young woman that had first attracted my attention. She had now completely disappeared. She was nowhere to be found.

After I got the contestants calmed down and seated in the auditorium, I took account of their losses, writing a check for each claim. Most of the contestants had obeyed instructions not to bring more than $5 to our rehearsals. But one contestant claimed to have lost $35. I gently reprimanded her, while writing a check for that amount.

Thankfully, only money was claimed. Still, the pageant went off well. We had a lovely queen.

The next morning, I turned on the TV at home and was completely shocked to see that the pageant robbery was the lead story of a local television news show! The entire page of contestant photos was spread across the television screen as the reporter announced:

"These teenage contestants were victims of a robbery last night during the Miss U. S. Talented Teens beauty pageant rehearsals held at Webster Hall in Oakland......"

I couldn't believe the station ran that report without first contacting me for verification. I was fuming. How dare they run that story without my input. I immediately called the television station.

"In all fairness, I should have been contacted for my side of the story," I said, angrily making my case to the station's news manager. "Those contestants were *immediately* reimbursed!"

"We won't run that piece again," the manager promised meekly. I hung up the phone, still fuming, seething with anger. Should I have demanded more of the station, the chance to tell my side of the incident on the next news hour? Yes, but I chose not to do so.

I reasoned that making a big fuss might bring unwanted attention to the incident. Strangely enough that had not happened. I was not besieged with phone calls from other media wanting more information, just silence. It was eerie, almost as though that story never ran.

*Certainly, God at work*

Later, I learned the TV reporter was the uncle of one of the contestants who had not placed in the competition. Not only that, but on a subsequent trip to New Jersey, visiting family, I saw that same reporter working in the area's smaller television news market. I wondered if he'd been fired because of his bad judgement in the Pittsburgh pageant story.

*Does not God work in mysterious ways?*

After that experience, I decided I would no longer produce Hal Jackson's Miss U. S. Talented Teen Pageant. Producing two pageants had become too stressful, too burdensome. Instead, I would concentrate on the Miss Black Teenage Pittsburgh pageant, now *my* pageant. I wanted it to become a major pathway to success for area young girls.

Meanwhile, despite a few bumps here and there, my marriage was going quite smoothly. But a knock on our door one hazy afternoon threatened to interrupt that tranquility. A young lady, a teenager, perhaps 16 years-old, appeared.

I want to speak to my father," she said almost defiantly. Surely, she had the wrong house, I thought. "Who is your father," I asked. "Mister Dewey," she replied. Now, I *had* to keep my wits about myself. Was I hearing right? Was this a joke?

"Who is your mother," I asked as calmy as possible. "Mary," (a fictitious name for privacy reasons) the girl answered somewhat innocently. "Well, he's asleep right now. I'll tell him you were here," I promised.

Oh yes! I kept that promise!

When Dewey awoke, I confronted him quietly, but my words were running together a mile-a-minute. "You never told me you had a daughter…. Her mother's name is "Mary," right? Well, your daughter was here to speak with you."

While Dewey was groggy when I first approached him, he became very alert when he heard what I had to say. He explained that the young girl was not his daughter but that of an old girlfriend. He further said the relationship was long over, but, he explained, he remained a father-figure to the girl.

I accepted his explanation. As a child of divorce, I understood the need for fatherly influence in one's life. But somehow, the name Mary, stayed with me. Little did I know that the sudden appearance of that young lady was, in fact, a harbinger of things to come. Her appearance was among a string of incidents that would bring about the end of our marriage.

Indeed, our marriage began to unravel rather quickly after that surprise visit. A few days after that visit, I arrived home after work to the smell of garlic and onions. I happily looked forward to the steak dinner that was immediately conjured up in my mind.

I made my way to the kitchen. But as I reached for the oven door to retrieve the dinner I thought Dewey had waiting for me, he held back my arm.

"Oh, no, Darling," he said. "I planned something else for us. We'll have a few drinks first and eat dinner out."

I stood perplexed as the thick smell of onions and garlic permeated the entire house. Before the night was over, I would have the answer to my wonderment.

We set out for drinks first at Dewey's favorite watering hole, a family bar, where – as in the sitcom "Cheers" – everybody knows your name. And, although I had never been there, everybody seemed to know my name.

We had barely been seated at the bar when a waitress, who was taking my order, exclaimed, "Miss Jean, your husband sure can cook. He cooked steaks for all of us today."

Aha! Murder will out, as they say. That explained the strong smell of garlic and onions I experienced earlier at home. Dewey was so fully engaged in conversation with the man seated on his left side, he was oblivious to what the waitress had just revealed to me.

I sat mystified as to why Dewey hadn't told me about his cooking expedition but I said nothing. There was something, however, I couldn't ignore: Strange, almost threatening stares were coming my way from The Woman in The Red Dress seated across the bar.

I motioned to the waitress that had taken our order for drinks. "Who is The Woman in The Red Dress?' I asked her.

"Oh, that's Mary," she answered with a modicum of innocence.

Mary! Something boiled up inside of me. I had an answer for what I now considered a challenge from Mary – The Woman in the Red Dress! Before I knew it, I grabbed Dewey, gave him a deep lingering kiss and turned to the Woman in the Red Dress to see if she got my message. I believe she nearly fainted. People seemed to be holding her up and fanning her.

Dewey, thoroughly embarrassed, escaped my embrace and quickly walked out, leaving his drink on the bar and me sitting alone. I tried to finish my drink but my hand was shaking uncontrollably. I set the glass down, steadied myself and walked out as well.

Dewey was waiting in the car. My mind was racing. I thought: "This is not the life I want to live. I didn't come more than 350 miles to contend with another woman." And I told Dewey as much as I got in the car.

We argued all the way on the drive home. Why did he not tell me he had cooked for everybody at the bar? Did he know Mary was going to be there? If there was nothing going on between them, why didn't he tell me who she was? Why did she go to such lengths, threatening stares and all, to make sure I noticed her?

Once home, Dewey answered at least one question. "I didn't know she would be there. I'm sorry," he said. I'm not sure I believed him. But I finally quieted down. I began to feel I had, perhaps, overreacted. Needless to say, the evening was spoiled for me. And though Dewey still wanted to take me out to dinner, I had no appetite. I sensed our marriage was slowly coming to an end.

One hot summer day a few months after the bar incident, I was working on a feature story at the newspaper. I took a break to call Dewey. Maybe I just wanted to hear his voice, to hear him call me *"Darling."* The phone was busy. I was disappointed but thought nothing of it and went back to work.

On the fourth try, I believed that maybe the phone was off the hook. The operator confirmed, however, there was conversation. That startled me. The line had been busy for more than an hour. Dewey always stressed that he rarely used the phone. So just who could he be talking to for so long?

A dark feeling of suspicion overcame me. Was he talking to Mary? Should I wait until he picks me up from work to ask? Do I have a right to know? Or should I ask the operator to break in knowing such a request is to be used only for true emergencies.

Since it was my lunch hour, I decided to play detective. I left the job and walked across the street to the Hilton Hotel, now the

Wyndham Grand Pittsburgh Downtown. I got a cab, gave the driver my address. So as not to be seen by Dewey, I got out at the corner near our home and walked the short distance to the house. I quietly turned the key in the front door, walked to the kitchen phone, and gently removed the receiver from its cradle.

As careful as I was, a crackling sound alarmed Dewey for a moment. He stopped talking. "What was that?" a female voice asked. Dewey shrugged it off and the conversation continued. The words he spoke next stunned me:

"Well, anyway, Darling, I love you and I always will."

I thought those words were reserved for me! But Dewey was speaking to someone else! My heart was beating so fast I felt it would leap from my chest! I couldn't believe my ears.

"So, who *is* this you love so much Dewey?" I yelled into the phone, slamming it back into the cradle and racing up the stairs to our bedroom. Dewey was so startled he was still holding onto the phone when I confronted him. He was lying comfortably across the bed in a white robe looking like the cat that ate the canary.

"You've been on the phone almost two hours while I tried to get you," my diatribe began, "*Who* were you talking to?"

Dewey remained silent as I ranted for a minute or two. He had a weak answer. "I was talking to a friend." He offered no name. And I didn't need one. I instinctively knew who it was. And I knew something else:

This was the end. There were many happy days during our marriage, yes, but distrust was a deal breaker. I was resolute in my thinking. When I quieted down, I asked Dewey to take me back to the Press. He did. We rode in silence, my thoughts racing through my brain. When we arrived at the Press, I pushed away from Dewey's attempted embrace and alighted from the car, saying in a very calm voice, "Don't bother to pick me up. I'm not coming home."

Back at the office, I checked the time. I'd been gone less than an hour and quickly got back to writing. On a break, I confided to a colleague what happened during my lunch hour and told her I planned to stay at the Hilton.

"You don't have to stay at a hotel." my colleague said. "You can stay with me and get yourself together." I accepted her gracious offer and stayed overnight in her apartment in Greentree, a Pittsburgh suburb. That night, she let me do all the talking. I needed to bare my soul and she accommodated me. The next morning, my colleague shared bagels and coffee with me and we drove to work together. I asked her if, after work, she could take me home to pick up some clothes and other personal items, then take me to the hotel.

After work, my colleague took me home as she promised. I knew Dewey would be working. I hurriedly filled my suitcase. When I went to get a few toiletries from the bathroom, I was startled to see a message written in red crayon across the width of the bathroom mirror:

"Darling, please come home."

For a moment, I wondered if I was acting too hastily, too rashly. But a knock at the door cut into my thoughts and I turned away from the message on the mirror. Dewey's oldest son, Tommy was my visitor. Did Dewey send him, I wondered.

Apparently not. Tommy seemed very surprised to see my hurriedly packed luggage in the middle of the living room floor. He asked me where I was going.

"I'm leaving your father. And I'm going to a hotel," I announced. "I'm waiting for Charles to come home from work." Charles by this time, was living with me and Dewey after being released from Lecumberri Prison in Mexico., where he had been held for some two years without charges and without a court date.

**(Please read Chapter Six: Charles Daniels for details)**

I'm sure he was unprepared for my response but he reacted swiftly. You can't stay at a hotel." Tom pleaded. He used the kitchen phone to call his mother, Martha. I didn't hear the conversation but he must have asked her if Charles and I could stay at their home. He was smiling when he reported to me.

"Mom said 'Tell Jean to come on!'"

I made a quick decision to accept Martha's charitable offer. I would be staying with Dewey's ex-wife, while looking for an apartment. What a true example of Christianity!

*God was at work again as always.*

Tommy drove me and Charles to Martha's home in Pittsburgh's Reserve Twp., a northern suburb, where she lived with her second husband Milton (Milt) Ward, their daughter, Sue and Thomas, Kenny and Richard, her sons with Dewey.

When I arrived at her home, Martha greeted me with a knowing hug, the kind of embrace that's full of compassion, that says, "I know what you've been through." Milt, a somewhat stocky man, stood by patiently waiting to be introduced. Then with a nod toward me, Tommy, Charles and Martha, he teased kiddingly:

"Hmmph! Looks like I've got Dewey's whole harem here."

In the ensuing days, I worked feverishly to find an apartment that would suit Charles and me. We didn't have to look long. It just happened that the apartment of a dear friend and colleague was immediately available. He had just accepted a job in Chicago with

Johnson Publications. He and his wife were ready and anxious to leave the area.

Their two-bedroom third-floor walk-up on Negley Avenue in Pittsburgh's East End area was perfect for Charles and me. It was right on the bus line and the 71A would get us fairly quickly Downtown to our jobs, mine at the Pittsburgh Press and his at the Gulf Oil Corporation.

*God is working overtime here.*

Almost immediately, the apartment was readied and Charles and I quickly moved in. We loved having the convenience of stepping practically from our front door onto a bus.

However, the daily 45-minute ride into town gave me too much time to think, too much time to question myself. Had I done the right thing by leaving Dewey? Had I overreacted? Should I call him and talk things over? He wasn't exactly bombarding me with calls.

By the time I arrived at Gateway Plaza, where the Press was located, I was convinced I had done the right thing. I would square my shoulders, put on my best smile for co-workers and get to work.

At the end of the day on the bus ride home, I always felt differently, saddened. My eyes would begin to well up with tears. I felt so alone. I thought so many people were going home to loved ones and here I sit going home to lonesomeness. I wore dark glasses to hide the tears.

I was pleased that the tenants in our building – a male cook from New York City on the first floor; a nurse on the second floor— seemed cordial enough. We all converged in the building at about the same time each evening. The light hearted banter between us seemed to cheer me up somewhat. And, so it went. Until one day, a few months after we moved in, a medical prescription I was waiting for didn't show up in my mail box.

My pharmacist assured me that he had mailed it out as he always did each month. But it never showed up. So, the pharmacist rushed a new prescription to me. A month later, it happened again. I was missing the prescription. Once again, my pharmacist insisted it had been mailed as usual.

On a hunch, Charles asked the New York tenant if he had seen it. Charles told me the man said he had not seen it. But Charles felt he was lying. I became suspicious also when a few days later, the tenant avoided eye contact with me in the lobby and quickly disappeared behind his apartment door.

In the meantime, the nurse moved out and the New York tenant's apartment flooded while he was away for a weekend. This called for a discussion with Charles about what I considered a necessary move – to a house not an apartment. Charles agreed. In our own home, we wouldn't need to worry about the trustworthiness of others.

That night, we mulled over the probable cost of purchasing a new home. We even considered moving back to New Jersey and all things familiar. Charles wasn't too anxious to leave Pittsburgh as he was happy with his new friends and his job in Gulf Oils' mailroom. But, he said, he would go along with whatever decision I made.

Sleep did not come easily as I turned and twisted all night long, restless with worry about the future. The next morning, as I rode the bus into town, I was filled with mixed emotions and depressing thoughts: I would soon be divorced. Why stay in Pittsburgh? No blood family here. What about the Miss Black Teenage pageant? I'd worked so hard to make it a first-class class event. Should I leave that behind?

As I approached Gateway Center that day, I looked upward and was suddenly captivated by the gleaming steel skyscrapers, the embodiment of Pittsburgh's Renaissance. Suddenly, I felt a strong surge of energy within me, energy fueled by the sun's rays dancing off the Gateway buildings.

I felt my own renaissance taking place.

*It had to be God*

I straightened my shoulders, took a deep breath and whispered to myself:

"This is going to be *my* town. I'm staying!"

I entered the Pittsburgh Press Building feeling pretty good about myself. I hadn't felt that way for some time. Months of indecision had worn me to a frazzle. But this new feeling, this confidence that suddenly gripped me gave me a sense of hope. Gone was that bleak, dreary outlook that plagued me in the months since I walked away from my marriage. I felt strong enough now to move forward, get on with my life.

Other than his scrawled message on the bathroom mirror, Dewey had made no attempt to contact me. I am sure that once he learned his ex-wife, Martha, had taken me in for a while, he knew I would not be coming back.

To cement my intentions to stay the course in Pittsburgh, I called on my good friend Carolyn Toney, who not only worked for PPG Industries in their building near the Pittsburgh Press, she also was a realtor in her spare time. Adding to that, she had become a true friend and a dedicated volunteer for my Miss Black Teenage pageant.

"I have a few homes to show you that I know you'll like," she told me. "It will just be a matter of which you like best."

That night, I shared my intent with Charles. He was in complete agreement and promised to help as much as he could financially. From that point on, Carolyn and I went house hunting. She was right. I liked most of the houses she showed me. But it wasn't until I laid eyes on the red brick three-bedroom split-level in Stanton Heights, that I knew I'd found my home, my ideal.

The house sits in an area on the eastern edge of the city. I call Stanton Heights "a suburb in the city." It became a place my New Jersey family loved to visit.

I played my cards right and got the house for a bargain - $10,000 less than the owner's asking price. I never let him see how anxious I was to buy. Instead, I focused on his need to sell quickly. He and his family had already moved to another township. And running back and forth between houses was wearing on him. Of course, he could have picked up his marbles and put the house back on the market. But, thank God, he didn't. Looking back, makes me break into a sweat. I almost overplayed my hand.

Charles surprised me by coming up with the $3,000 for closing fees, savings I had no idea he had. On July 15, 1979, the closing was held, all fees were paid, and we were at once the owners of the home I fell in love with at first sight.

*God is good*

Once settled in my new home, I felt a renewed sense of belonging, a deep sense of commitment to my neighborhood and to the greater community that had supported me and my programs for the past seven years.

Within three months after moving in, I was approached about helping to organize a block Club. I became its first president. Joyce Meggerson-Moore, PhD, who lived near me, served as vice president. About three years later, Joyce and I served in the same capacities for the Stanton Heights Community Organization (SHCO), which evolved from the block club.

For the next 20 years, with a very supportive membership and community, Joyce and I led the fight to maintain the stability of our residential area. As SHCO officials, we fought off developers after developers who wanted to commercialize our neighborhood. They all had their eyes fixed on the 23 acres of woodland in our community, that stretched from along our back yards to Stanton Avenue and beyond.

All manner of wild life – deer, red fox, racoons, rabbits and birds – lived on those acres. Developers and their lawyers had plans for that area that didn't include these beautiful animals. They wanted to clear the woodlands to make way for a shopping mall and an apartment complex.

We were besieged by men in pin stripped suits and black wing-tip shoes, carrying fat brief cases. Residents, whose homes bordered on or were near the woodlands, objected to the prospect of tearing down this greenery and losing the tranquility they enjoyed to a noisy, high-traffic mall.

In meetings with these men, I deliberately wore a black-pin-striped suit and carried my own briefcase as well. But that didn't stop one developer from addressing me thusly: "Listen honey," he began. I stopped him cold. "I'm *not* your honey!" I shot at him to his chagrin and embarrassment. His face turned beet red as he beat a hasty retreat, apologizing profusely.

SHCO chased them all away, until eventually the word went out to developers– so I was told – that to make any progress, you had to "get past Jean Bryant and that woman who wears the braids," referring to Joyce Meggerson-Moore.

They finally did get past us. A city council member, who constantly opposed SHCO, helped organize a new group, gave it a name similar to ours and gained enough influence to end SHCO'S 20-year history of keeping developers at bay and our precious woodland intact.

A high school, a high-rise for the elderly and a Kingdom Hall for Jehovah's Witnesses now occupy the land.

SHCO did not oppose the Kingdom Hall. We can take credit now for the fact that the threat of a shopping mall or a large apartment complex no longer exists.

Although things seemed to be going smoothly in my life, I became concerned that my job status might be changing. In 1991, the Teamsters Union, Local 211, and Press Management began butting heads. When they couldn't come to agreement on a new contract, the Teamsters walked off the job, resulting in an eight-month strike.

Was I worried about my job? Yes. Another big worry for me then was my investment portfolio. I got a call from a PNC Bank official with news I considered disturbing. He said he would no longer be handling my 401K, that I would receive an official letter from the bank and a call from Jeff Gray, my new financial advisor. What did all this mean I wondered.

The call from Jeffrey and a later meeting with him at once eased my fears. And, later, at a time when the climate was looking gloomy for investment portfolios, Jeff called me with good news.

"I found an investment opportunity that includes a bonus offer for new investors," he said. "You will receive a cash bonus in excess of $8,000!"

*God keeps blessing me!*

My portfolio continued to thrive under Jeff's guidance, which allowed me to continue underwriting with confidence the costs of my pageant productions. Jeff retired March 1, 2021.

Meanwhile, after the strike, E. W. Scripps, owners of the Press, sold the paper to The Pittsburgh Post-Gazette. It was a sad time for many of my former colleagues, some of whom left the city to find work. Fortunately, others were hired by our rival newspaper, the Pittsburgh Tribune-Review. I was blessed to be one of those hired by the Pittsburgh Post-Gazette.

*God is still blessing me!*

Chapter Five:

# Pageantry

My Passion

Miss Black Teenage (MBT)

Mister African American (MAA)

"GOOD MORNING, LADIES. I HAVE to say, I believe the most beautiful young women in Pittsburgh are right here in this room!"

That is how I greeted participants each Saturday morning at rehearsals for (MBT) in 1973, the year the pageant was launched in the Steel City. Those words never changed during the 35 years I produced the pageant.

MBT became one of the most widely supported and recognized programs for young black ladies in the region. Just as much attention was given to my later program for young black men, called, Mister African American (MAA).

Over a 35-year period, I awarded more than $500,000 in educational scholarships to contestants in various categories. Graduates have gone on to become recognizable and honored members of the judicial system, entertainment industry, media and associations of professionals.

Their successes are a source of immense joy and pride to me. When I started producing MBT, first as a Hal Jackson franchise and later as my own enterprise, I worried if the young ladies and their parents would be interested, if they would actually show up. That first day of rehearsal in 1971 in New Jersey and in 1973 in Pittsburgh proved the skeptics wrong. The success of the MBT program and, later MAA, exceeded my wildest expectations. I have been just as blessed by that success as were the contestants.

Pittsburgh's first Miss Black Teenage Queen Renee Moore,
ends reign, crowns new queen, Lisa Ruffin

My morning greeting to those young ladies was sincere. How could it not be? They were beautiful. And they came wanting to look their best. They wanted to improve each week as they learned how to dress for success, care for their skin, how to walk gracefully, how to sit properly, how to introduce themselves sincerely on a job interview. Though the age range was 13 to 17 years old, they all received the same level of instruction and each soaked up the knowledge they were receiving.

I could tell from their smiles that they welcomed being told how beautiful they were. Seeing their receptiveness, reminded me how exuberant the ladies had been when we called them at their homes on evenings, after morning interviews, to tell them they had been accepted as contestants. Their screams of joy, "I made it!" could be heard by whoever was listening, including those of us on the other end of the phone.

Each year, hearing those delightful screams, reinforced my promise that MBT contestants would never regret their experience. I wanted them to know that they had been nurtured by people who cared about them, who wanted them to be the best they could be and who had treated them fairly.

I wanted to make each contestant feel as though she was among family, that she was loved. I wanted their experience to be something they would remember always. It would be something of a keepsake.

Apparently, we succeeded at that. Often throughout the years, contestants entered the competition more than once.

One such lovely family of former contestants included the Barbour sisters. Andrea Barbour entered twice (1984 and 1985); Jennifer Barbour entered four times, (1985, 1986, 1987 and 1989); and Kelly Barbour Ramsey entered three times, (1988, 1989 and 1990). She won the Most Talented award in 1990.

Andrea and Jennifer Barbour are now the owners of the Ms. Ann and Ms. Jen's Piano and Tutoring Center in Green Tree.

Other former contestants entered their own children or entered relatives. Many former contestants continued their involvement as judges or volunteers or came back to share their successes with current contestants.

*God is good always.*

We typically began accepting applications for the pageant in January. Our focus would be on *inclusion* not *exclusion*, something they may face too often in life. Therefore, as many as applied might be accepted.

One instance, however, caused an application to be rejected. The picture attached to the application was much too suggestive. I sent it back with a stern letter. The applicant actually called me, asking forgiveness. But not knowing her background, I felt I could not relent, although some committee members felt I should have.

Our Saturday rehearsals – usually in a school, church or community center – followed a typical format. After my morning greeting, contestants lined up according to numbers assigned them. They practiced walking as if wearing a gown, and rehearsed 15-second speeches, introducing themselves to the judges.

Afterwards, a Word for the Day – incorporated into the program – was discussed as to how such a creed could be helpful in their everyday lives.

Among my favorites were *the journey of a thousand miles, begins with the first step*, which I frequently used to stress that MBT was a first step on their journey to success. And the motto *Don't put off until tomorrow, what you can do today* was helpful in pointing out that waiting until the last minute to perfect their performances was not a good idea.

For lack of space, contestants usually remained in their seats at lunch time. It was a fun time as they ate and got to know each other. Conversations were lively and laughter was constant as they forged relationships. After lunch, scheduled speakers lectured 30 minutes on teen issues, then everyone's talent was reviewed and critiqued.

The rules in MBT were strict. Every rule had a purpose. Sneakers were not allowed nor were jeans. Only dresses or a skirt and blouse were accepted at rehearsals. Contestants could be sent home if they broke the rules. The loss of even one day at rehearsals could significantly impact their chance of winning the crown. The goal was to help them understand appropriateness in dress wear, such as no low decollete on gowns or dresses, no mini dresses or mini-skirts.

I continually worked at making MBT better in every way possible. Some rules were standard. For instance, only two excused absences from rehearsals were allowed. Contestants had to take the program seriously, understand how important their attendance was for a smooth-running production.

There were three important segments for each show: The Appearance & Personality segment in which each contestant appears before judges and the audience wearing her gown and introduces herself in a 15-second speech; the Talent Segment, limited to 2 minutes, and the Question & Answer Segment, during which all previous votes from judges have been eliminated. The winner of the most points from this segment is determined the queen.

To ensure fairness, a 15-second limit was placed on the speeches, so older contestants had no advantage over younger contestants. Also, I wanted our young ladies to start thinking about their futures so each speech had to contain a desired goal. (I edited and – in most cases – rewrote each speech to make sure it adhered to the time limit and was written to impress).

And to ensure fairness in judging, preliminary judges – whose votes determine the 15 finalists – and finals judges were always a completely different set of people. Neither set of judges will have seen the contestants beforehand.

Then, comes Thursday Night Rehearsal at Soldiers and Sailors Memorial Hall. It is always three days before the Mother's Day event. It's the very first time the young ladies get to stand on the Big Stage in the auditorium. It is on this night they get last instructions for their big night.

We always relaxed the dress code for Thursday Night Rehearsals. I announce the instructions for this important evening. "We will do this rehearsal as if it is the night of the pageant, no coaching, no corrections. If you forget anything, keep going. No starting over."

Pageant Night! What could compare to the excitement of Pageant Night, which was always held on Mother's Day at Soldiers and Sailor Memorial Hall. The hall was the home of both MBT and MAA. It's wide stage and enormous back stage area make it, in my opinion, Pittsburgh's most perfect place to hold a pageant or competition of any sort.

**Charles Sings 0n pageant night**

By that night, we would have done all we could to help each girl reach her greatest potential: Dancers got personal attention from dance coaches, orators got personal attention from drama coaches, singers got personal attention from singing coaches and instrumentalists got personal attention as well. The dedicated coaches came from area churches and schools to share their expertise with the contestants and help the girls hone their skills. Most of these coaches returned year after year.

In preparation for Pageant Night, contestants were rehearsed eight weeks on how to walk in their gowns; they were schooled on likely questions regarding currents events for the Question & Answer segment.

For me, nothing could match the thrill of Pageant Night, of watching contestants appear either from behind the hall's back stage area into the auditorium where the pageant was, or, from the hall's outer lobby into the auditorium. Family members, fans, my team and I waited breathlessly for that dramatic entrance.

Each year this annual procession of gowned young women amazed me! It was like having carefully seeded a garden of lovely flowers and suddenly seeing the buds explode into their full beauty.

Once all contestants are on stage, they sing in unison a current popular song. It is then announced "Ladies and Gentlemen. The Miss Black Teenage Contestants!

A second announcement: "Yesterday, our Preliminary judges voted here in Soldiers and Sailors Memorial Hall. Their votes have decided who the 15 finalists are!" One by one the finalists are called by name and contestant number. A loud drum-roll behind each name heightens the tension. And at this time. I am always at the edge of my seat.

And, from my front-row seat, hearing those beautiful young women express their hopes and dreams in a 15-second speech, I just knew this was not the end but the beginning of a journey filled with hope and achievements. I knew that I would hear of their accomplishments, and possibly, the world would hear of them too.

My concept, my rationale for my pageantry venture went like this:

"Shakespeare says, 'All the world is a stage.' I say, we will give them the stage and they will conquer the world."

On February 28. 1993 – in response to queries as to why no such competition existed for young black males – I developed the Mister African American (MAA) program for ages 13 to 17. It also encompassed a segment – Mister African American Junior – for boys nine to 11 years old.

MAA would be my pride and joy for different reasons. I envisioned a program that would feed the young men a huge dose of their ancient history as being descendants of kings and queens. I wanted to fill them with a sense of pride and hope. Ronald B. Saunders, an expert in Black history, who was named one of the New Pittsburgh Courier's 50 Men of Excellence for 2021, was charged with teaching Black History to our young men. Elbert Hatley, then director of the Hill Community Development Corp., and LaMont Jones Jr., former Pittsburgh Post-gazette news reporter/columnist and a minister, handled the rest of the curriculum.

I wrote a creed for MAA contestants to follow, hopefully, for a life time: *"As a young African-American male, I pledge to show respect for God, myself, my family, my neighborhood and the greater community. I also pledge to teach this creed to those who are younger and I promise to give back to my community in positive ways."*

Imagine a stage full of handsome young black males dressed in tuxedos and saying this pledge in unison. It was the program's Opening Number for the next ten years, until the program ended in November 2002.

In 1993, when the MAA program began, gangs like the Crips and Bloods were prevalent in Pittsburgh's urban areas. It was a worrisome time for young boys. I consulted my son Crawford, by then a retired Orange, N. J. policeman, about hiring security for MAA rehearsals.

"No Mom, you won't need to do that," he said. "You'll be sending the wrong message to them." I took Crawford's advice. I'm glad I did. I felt he was absolutely right.

Why should they be made to feel they needed policing? The nearest thing to a problem happened when one contestant ate another's lunch. But once the culprit confessed, Behavior Monitor Earlina Williams took both boys aside, got them to shake hands and saw that both boys ate.

That incident, however, brought to my attention something that was at once troubling to me. Although bringing a lunch was required in both programs, several MAA contestants went without, substituting candy bars for what should have been a nutritious meal. I pondered the question, are the needs of our young black males treated indifferently by their families, by society? So, to ensure the young men had lunch, volunteers often shared their own lunches with them.

Since we understood many MAA applicants might not have a suit or dress shoes, we relaxed the dress code. We didn't want to lose a single applicant for dress code reasons. We met them where they were, so to speak. Jeans and sneakers were allowed. However, to set examples of what success looks like, male volunteers were required to wear suits.

I wanted these young men to become polished gems. With that goal in mind, I decided tuxedos would become the uniform for the program without cost to participants. I wanted all the young men to know how good it felt to be dressed up, to be looking good and feeling good.

What amazed me was how carefully the young men treated the tuxedos. It was as if they knew that, in wearing the tuxedos, they were experiencing something special, perhaps a once in a lifetime event.

I had arranged to rent the tuxedos from a local shop. The young men attended fittings at the shop on time, picked up their tuxedos on time and returned them to the store on time.

One year, a frightening incident happened when the tuxedo store I'd been dealing with, suddenly declared bankruptcy and I had to find another rental store. On the eve of the show when all the contestants had been fitted at the new location, the owner refused to accept my $1,500 check. He wanted cash before the young men could leave with the merchandise. He was not impressed with my credentials.

"I don't care *who* you are. Cash only!"

I was frenzied. The hour was late. No banks were open. Who could I call for help on a $1,500 bill?

But a patron in the shop observed my dilemma and quietly stepped forward. "I *know* who you are. I've been to your shows. Write the check out to me. I'll pay him with my credit card."

Unbelievable! Yes! If ever in my lifetime, I was speechless this has to be the moment! I thanked him profusely as I wrote the check for the amount of the bill.

*God working over-time again!*

As the years rolled by, I developed new ideas for both programs: bigger cash scholarship awards for the winners, from $500 to $1,000. Even the committee became involved in personally sponsoring cash awards such as Best Singer, Best Gown, Best Attendance, Best Talent. I added a $2,000 Continuing Education Scholarship for those who would go on to earn masters or doctorate degrees.

However, the most incredulous development of all happened when former contestant Traci McDonald, of Washington, PA – a Clarion University graduate, became its Assistant Director of Admissions. Traci used her position to initiate an agreement with Clarion that provided *four-year tuition-free scholarships* to the MBT and MAA programs.

*God is good!*

That arrangement helped Clarion boost its diversity goals, and we were able to provide a tuition-free college education to our program participants who were seeking higher education.

When Traci left Clarion for other pursuits, Gemma

Stemley, already a Clarion employee, stepped in to replace her. Gemma kept the alliance between Clarion and my programs in place until my retirement in 2008.

As time went on, I became even bolder with entertainment ideas. One year, for the MBT show, I had body-builders appear in a short segment wherein they demonstrated the different poses used in competition. That took the cake! Women, mothers were shouting their approval, and practically falling out of their seats, pulling out their cameras at the sight of the well-oiled, well sculptured bodies on stage. I remembered thinking, "I hope they remember to save film for their daughters."

Another time, I presented two white teen table- tennis champs in an amazing exhibition of exceptional skill. The audience loved it. As the years rolled by, and participation grew, I began to concentrate on ways to shorten the length of the pageant without sacrificing its uniqueness. We cut out the extra entertainment and shortened customary break time.

I began to include our program graduates and our college graduates as judges, lecturers and as volunteers for our MBT/MAA programs. Very often, parents of former participants became faithful volunteers and committee members. Some served as long as 35 years until the pageant came to a close in 2008, a very sad day for me.

I was 76 years old, no longer possessed with the vim and vigor required to produce two youth programs. But the memories are plentiful – some heart breaking, sorrowful. Others, joyous, unforgettable.

One unforgettable memory is the year that a 16-year-old white teenager sat among contestants waiting to be interviewed for acceptance in the MBT pageant. We wondered how to tell her the pageant was for black girls.

"Oh, I'm not here to be in the pageant, I'm here as a sponsor," she explained. Indeed, she sponsored and attended every rehearsal for Ruth Featherstone, a 15-year-old, with a powerful voice in the tradition of gospel legend, Mahalia Jackson.

At the last rehearsal, when we usually ask contestants for comments on the program, Rose stood up to speak.

"I just want to say this program gave me the confidence to do something I always dreamed of doing but my brother told me I could never do. I joined the U. S Army!"

Rose came back to visit and address contestants the next year wearing her U. S. Army uniform. Ruth Featherstone is now an accomplished gospel singer and has her own ministry Sunday mornings on Facebook and You Tube.

Another young lady's testimony made me extremely happy. When asked what she liked most about the Miss Black Teenage Program, she said she loved learning table etiquette best.

"It made me feel rich," she said with a broad smile.

While those memories warm my heart, another memory saddens me:

One year, a contestant would not look out to the audience or smile as instructed when appearing on stage. Instead, she turned away from the audience. Since my practice was to never be alone with a contestant, I signaled for assistance from contestant aide, Penny Walker. Together we pulled the young lady aside and questioned her about why she refused to look at the audience. "Because I'm ugly," she blurted out. I was shocked to the core, speechless. Of course, we had a long talk with her, shoring up her self-confidence.

In another instance, a contestant kept talking back to volunteer Charlene Grigsby, who had to constantly remind the young lady to sit quietly while programming was in progress. Finally, Charlene brought the contestant to me and Pageant Coordinator Gwen Moore.

When asked why she talked back to our volunteer, she answered defiantly: "I talk to my mother that way." "You do," I asked incredulously "why?"

"Because she didn't believe me when I told her I was raped! Other people had to help me," she answered, near tears.

I quietly asked for permission to hug her. She nodded "yes." We clung together for a moment and I could feel the animosity draining from her as she realized we were not the enemy.

I asked what happened to her attacker. "He did time in jail but he's out now," she said.

"Listen, you're being miserable while he's going on with his life," I told her. Gwen suggested she get help and gave the young lady some ideas before she went back to her seat. The young lady was a model of good behavior for the duration of our program. At the last rehearsal, when contestants were asked for comments on the pageant experience, this young lady was the first to stand. Her comments had the pageant committee near tears:

"First, I want to apologize to all the contestants and all the committee members for my past actions. I'm truly sorry," she began. "And I want to know why this program only lasts for eight weeks?"

I was choked up! This young lady did what many adults can't bring themselves to do – apologize or even acknowledge they did anything to apologize for. And she wanted the program to go on for longer than the scheduled eight weeks!

I think of her often because her short speech told me what I needed to know, that I was on the right track with programming, with our philosophy to affirm each contestant's beauty, give them structure, listen to them.

Her ability to express regret for her past behavior brought home to me how so many teens are silently hurting and just need someone to listen to them. Of course, we couldn't fix all the contestants' problems, but what we *could* do was to make them feel good about themselves, give them something wonderful to remember, something that centered around them, a beautiful event, a keepsake of sorts. We gave them Confidence, Awareness and Pride, the pageant motto.

In yet another instance, local lawyer Cliff Cooper approached me at a social event with news that completely startled me.

"Your program helped me win a court case," he said with a grin. Cliff went on to explain that a client brought her daughter to his office wanting to bring charges against a police officer for assaulting the girl.

"I took one look at the young lady and told her mother there's *no way* I can defend *her*."

The girl had a tough demeanor, a defiant attitude, Cooper said. When the woman pleaded with him to take the case, he said he made a deal with her:

"Put her in the Miss Black teenage pageant. Then, bring her back to me."

All during the eight weeks of rehearsal, I had absolutely no knowledge of what was happening or who the young lady was.

Cliff said the girl and her mom returned to his office after the pageant. He said he was more than pleased with her appearance and her new attitude. They went to court.

"The judge could not believe the cop threw this dainty young girl into a wall. He found for the defendant! I won the case!"

Over the years, the corps of volunteers and committee members grew substantially, most were parents of former contestants. Not so, 16-year-old Kevin Smith. In 1981, he was the pianist for contestant Sheila Green. At a rehearsal that year, young Kevin approached me during a lull in programming.

"Mrs. Bryant, I like what you're doing and I'd like to be a part of it," he said. Indeed, for the next 27 years, Kevin served MBT as a pianist for contestants who were without an accompanist. He also played during intervals in the show until 2008, when the program ended.

There are so many success stories among our former MBT/MAA participants. They are leading   successful lives from California, Alaska to New York City and Washington, D. C. I can't name them all but I'd like to mention several most recent of whom I am most proud.

**Traci McDonald Kemp,** On January 4, 2016, Traci, a former Miss Black Teenage participant, who initiated free four-year scholarships for our MBT/MAA programs, became **the first African-American female elected to the bench in Washington County, PA.**

**Kendra Ross**, PhD, a 1989 Miss Black Teenage participant, is **Assistant Professor of Sports, Arts and Entertainment management at Point Park University and a partner in Act3 Consultants with Denelle Biggs**, also a former Miss Black Teenage participant, and Tanika Harris.

**Melanie (Hunter) Arter**, a 1989-1991 Miss Black Teenage participant, is **White House Correspondent and Senior Editor for CSNNews.com.**

**Luther J. Dupree, Jr.,** a 1993 Mister African American participant, was named as one of the **New Pittsburgh Courier's 50 Men of Excellence for 2021.** He is Founder/Director of Steel City Sports World. He is   also a service coordinator for Pittsburgh Mercy.

**Brian Cook**, a 1997 Mister African American participant, is Owner, Photographer, and Videographer of Golden Sky Media. **He also is a Contributing Producer at WQED Pittsburgh and is President of the Pittsburgh Black Media Federation.**

**Dr. Ruth Andrea Featherstone**, a 1979 Miss Black Teenage participant, has honorary doctorates in Sacred Music and **delivers**

"Sunday Worship Experience with Dr. Ruth Andrea Featherstone" at 8 p.m. on **Facebook and You Tube.**

**Jillian Woodruff Gay, MD,** a former Miss Black Teenage contestant, **who struck out on her own and set up offices specializing in obstetrics and gynecology in Anchorage, Alaska, where she lives with her husband Dr. Christopher Gay and their two children.**

Pageant Committee

Chapter Six:

# Our Four Sons

RAISING FOUR HEALTHY BOYS – Crawford, Stephen, Bernard, and Charles – was a joy. They were fun, handsome and – for the most part – well-mannered and well-behaved. Each, however, developed his own personality along life's way.

Four sons in bed L to R Crawford, Charles, Bernard, and Stephen

Crawford was empathetic and caring. Stephen was more practical and business-minded, a leader. Bernard was kind-hearted, a follower, while Charles, the shortest among them, had what I determined to be a Napoleonic complex.

Throughout the children's early childhood and high school years, we lived on Ward Street in Orange, N. J. And later, on Heywood Avenue in the Seven Oaks area of Orange.

To have lost my four sons –Bernard in 1999 of colon cancer; Crawford in 2018 of heart failure, Charles in 2019 of stage four prostate cancer and Stephen of kidney-related illnesses in 2021 while still young adults has been beyond devasting to me and our family. It put me in such a dark, dark place. And, for a while, I didn't think I would ever smile again. I didn't want to live. Why would I?

But a lovely sympathy card counseled: "While grieving, look back, not forward." I did that and quickly realized God had been there for me all along: I saw my children become young men, I was able to buy a home that, in their later years, became a refuge for them. Now, they are with God. No more pain, no more suffering. God's promise that we will see each other again, eases my torment and gives me comfort and peace.

I have given each of my four sons a chapter in this book because I believe their stories are unique. It is a sort of memorial to their lives.

## Crawford S. Daniels

Crawford Solon entered this world September 13, 1947 at St Elizabeth Hospital, Elizabeth, N. J. His middle name was in honor of my step-father, Daniel Solon Pinkett.

As a young man, Crawford's empathy for others had no boundaries. He was always concerned for the plight of others, a soft touch, often to his detriment. He was quick to come to the aid of those he thought were being treated unfairly, or who just needed a helping hand.

One of my most vivid memories is of Crawford's first fisticuffs. To my knowledge, Crawford had not been in any kind of row with schoolmates or neighborhood kids. And I never imagined that at six years-old he would be the target of a neighborhood bully.

Teddy was a rough-and-tumble-tough-as-nails six-year-old white kid. He lived near our Ward Street home and played with kids twice his age.

Younger kids feared Teddy. And, apparently, the bow ties and neat suits Crawford wore to school made Teddy think Crawford could be easily intimidated.

One summer day in 1953, the sound of Crawford's plaintive voice wafted through my second-story kitchen window.

"Give me my money back, Teddy," Crawford pleaded. "Take it!" Teddy dared him.

I was shocked and stunned at what was happening to my six-year-old. Teddy was the same age, but a bit taller than Crawford and somewhat heavier. I knew what was in store for Crawford. I had seen for myself how tough Teddy was when I witnessed how he had been dealt with at home.

On my way to a store close to his home several months earlier, I observed an incident between Teddy and his father. His father, obviously angry and appearing somewhat inebriated, used his tightly balled fist to give Teddy a harsh blow to the forehead. Teddy hit the ground, never a tear, not a sound. He just got up and walked away, head down.

I gasped. I felt sorry for Teddy but kept going. I never met the family and feared getting involved. Now, this seemingly fearless kid was confronting Crawford, who was, by comparison, a pretty gentle soul. I couldn't tear myself from the window. Things were happening too fast

"Take your money, Crawford," I yelled. When Crawford stepped forward to grab it, Teddy gave him a big shove backwards.

"Push him back," I yelled, still afraid to leave the window. Somehow, Crawford found the strength. He pushed back with all his might. They both fell to the ground.

"Crawford, get on top! …Take your money!" I was frantic. Finally, Crawford straddled Teddy, got his money back and sent Teddy packing.

"You did good!" I called down to Crawford as he stifled the urge to cry. "It's alright. Go ahead and cry," I reassured him. As soon as those words left my lips, my little man ran to the back of our house and let out a loud cry. "Waah!"

Victory was not so sweet.

I was still standing at the kitchen window, when an older white gentleman, appeared below. He had not witnessed the beginnings of the tussle between Crawford and Teddy but had heard my loud prompting. He looked up and began wagging a finger at me.

"You should be ashamed of yourself!" He called up to me. "He tried to take my son's money. I yelled back."

I recognized him as the neighbor who lived several doors away. I jokingly referred to him as "The Mayor of Ward Street" because he seemed to be everywhere, watching everything. After our exchange, he shook his head and continued on his way.

Needless to say, however, Teddy made it a point to avoid Crawford. There were no more skirmishes between them.

During his teen to manhood years in Orange, Crawford would become many things: an all-around athlete at Orange High School

– basketball, football, baseball, boxing and track. He earned the nickname, "Shoes" because by the time he was an upper classman at OHS, he was wearing a size 12 shoe.

He became a community activist, published "Black Oranges," a community newsletter and worked to make peace between the Black and Italian community. He also joined the New Jersey National Guard (1968- 1978) and was a member of the Orange Police Department (1974- 1995 )

Crawford also won several awards, including the Orange/East Orange Optimist Club Service Award, given to, "A Police Officer Who Serves the Community and is Dedicated to Improving the Lives of Youth."

Most surprisingly, he became a budding playwright. "I Am" (2013), "Eugene Tillman" (2014) and "Just a "Damn Dog" (2015). He was a major financial contributor to the Orange YWCA, The Oranges/Maplewood NAACP, The Urban League, The Big "O" Booster Club and several other local programs.

He would also become the father of daughters Toni and Keisha Baker, Andaiye Wylie and Khadijah Harrison and a father-figure to Terri Baker.

When the need arose, Crawford stepped forward to care for two other children in our family, Samad Daniels, the son of a cousin, Christopher Daniels and Daralyn Corprew, the daughter of Crawford's younger brother, Bernard.

Twice, Crawford experienced run-ins with police bent on skull-duggery. The first incident occurred in East Orange, a neighboring town, where he stopped his car curbside so a lady friend could alight.

A policeman approached, ordering him to "Keep moving!" Crawford refused to move until he deemed his lady friend was safely out of the car.

That got Crawford his first arrest. It got the police captain a letter from me criticizing the arrest, in part saying that: "The arresting officer was not wearing a hat and took no note that a young lady was stepping out of the car at the time."

The letter got me an invitation to meet with the police captain. "Oh-oh," I thought.

Shortly after the incident, I arrived at the police station and was taken to the captain's office. He entered a few minutes later, smiling. "I *had* to meet the mother who wrote this letter," he said. Embolden, I gave the captain an earful of suggestions for better policing. Crawford's charges were dismissed. The captain and I shook hands. "I wish all mothers would write letters like this," he said.

*God is good!*

Crawford's second encounter with police was horrible, horrific and could have been deadly! It happened in Newark, several miles from our Ward Street home. His empathetic nature was in full display.

He was in line with a lady friend at a popular White Castle restaurant when he saw Newark policemen beating a young man he recognized. He left the line and went to plead with police to stop beating his friend, a co-worker. The cops turned their wrath on Crawford, threw them both in a patrol car and drove off.

I got the call for help from Crawford's lady friend. I raced to Newark police station and demanded to see my son. The desk sergeant denied my request. So, from a station phone booth, I made a frenzied call to Sharpe James, then a Newark city Councilman. I knew James because The Soul Dukes had performed at several of James' campaign rallies.

**RET. OFFICER CRAWFORD S. DANIELS**
City Of Orange, N.J.
Police Department

- Orange High School Graduate
- Attended University of Tennessee, at Knoxville
- Devoted Son, Brother, Father, Grandfather, Uncle, Nephew
- Family Historian
- Loving
- Caring (Raised four children, plus three more not his own)
- Humanitarian
- Philanthropist
- Patron of the Arts
- Playwright, "I Am:" "Eugene Tillman"
- Community Acivist
- Publisher-Owner, "Black Oranges News"
- US Chess Federation Member, Teacher
- Avid Reader
- Friend of both Orange and East Orange Libraries
- Member, Orange "Y:" Major Donor
- Member, Orange NAACP, Major Donor

*Rest in Peace, my beautiful son,*
*Jean Bryant*

After we hung up, James called the precinct and instructed the sergeant there to allow me to see Crawford. James called me back. "I told him to let you see your son or, I'll be down there in my pajamas," he said.

Crawford and Eugene Tillman, the young man he tried to rescue, were brought out together and seated on a bench in the police station lobby. It was surreal. Their faces were bloodied, eyes swollen and heads misshapen from unmerciful blows.

I screamed bloody murder.

"What have you done to my son!?"

Years later, Crawford wrote the play, "Eugene Tillman," about this beating at the hands of Newark police. The play debuted May 12, 2014 at The Second Annual Short Play Festival at Luna Stage, West Orange, N. J. Nine writers presented their works at the festival. After Crawford presented his play, he received the only standing ovation of the evening. I was never so proud.

Crawford's charitable nature came into play at the University of Tennessee, Knoxville, which he attended two years. Some students quickly learned they could count on Crawford for help when they were low on funds. His father and I sent him a monthly allowance that we thought would tide him over during his school years. I worried that we weren't sending him enough money.

But at the end of his first year when we called Crawford to find how much he needed for airfare home, he astonished me. "I don't need any money…I'm collecting from loans I made," he said. So, I worried for nothing. We had sent him enough money, after all.

Crawford also loaned money to his high school buddies when he worked for his dad at Daniels' Auto Body Shop, which was located on a corner near our home. In one instance, he actually signed for a loan, twice, for a childhood friend. The friend defaulted on both loans. Crawford got stuck each time.

"When will you ever learn, Crawford?" I asked him.

But two things, in my opinion, became over-riding factors later in Crawford's outlook on life – unrequited teen love and the later death of his first child, Toni Marie. A registered nurse, Toni carried my middle name. She died of breast cancer just before her 40th birthday. While we all mourned Toni's loss, her death hit Crawford particularly hard and he went into a deep depression.

His first major heart break occurred when he was a 15-year-old teenager. Crawford fell hard for the girl of his dreams. Joan and Crawford attended Orange High School together. She lived just two doors away. Still, Crawford rode his bike daily to her front door. It was summer. They would chat for hours, she on her porch steps and he astride his bike.

But suddenly someone else came along, stole her heart. Crawford never saw it coming, Things changed quickly. Joan married her new love. They had a child. Joan died soon after child-birth.

Crawford never talked about losing Joan to someone else. I remember the sadness in his eyes. I wish now that I had approached him about it. But I felt I might have embarrassed him if I brought it up. I thought he would eventually confide in me. He never did.

While I believe lost love was one reason Crawford never married, I also believe he was impacted by the discord he witnessed between me and his father.

In time, Crawford seemed to put these disappointments behind him. Instead of brooding, he began volunteering to help others. Through his work at the Orange YWCA, he organized and coached basketball games for the city's young women as well as for adult men in the city. He became a member of both the Orange and East Orange Public Libraries and taught chess for both institutions.

The family was dealt a major blow when in February 2015, Crawford, then 67, suffered a stroke at his home in Orange. He was found by his young cousin Samad (who he helped raise) and rushed by ambulance to nearby Mountainside Hospital in Montclair. He was treated there and released to Kessler Rehabilitation Institute in West Orange, N. J. The stroke left him with loss of peripheral vision in his left eye, slightly slurred speech and he could no longer distinguish between certain numbers.

After his release from Kessler, Crawford came to live with me in Pittsburgh, where we all hoped for a full recovery.

Among Crawford's medical records, I discovered a copy of a questionnaire he filled out for Kessler. It revealed how mentally tortured Crawford really was, how dark his world had become. It also revealed he was self-medicating.

Learning these things devastated me. He declined all help for these problems while living with me in Pittsburgh.

Crawford had been with me three years when he decided to get back to Orange, the hometown he loved so much. While he made good use of his time in Pittsburgh – he joined Vintage Community Center, enrolled in two different Bible-study classes, taught chess and made a host of friends – something was missing for him.

He ached to get back to Orange to *his* alma mater, *his* community. He *had* to leave. There was no changing Crawford's mind. I felt he wasn't ready. He was still having problems distinguishing certain numbers, critical for using a microwave for meals, for example.

Nevertheless, Crawford had applied for and been approved for an apartment on the eighth floor in a Senior Citizens high-rise next to Orange Park, the scene of many family picnics during his childhood.

His brother, Charles, and I, saw him off on Amtrak in October 2018. My heart was heavy when we hugged and said "Good bye."

Ten months after he left, Crawford was hospitalized again. He had fallen while bathing and could not get out of the bathtub. He was able to use a help-button to alert building personnel and an ambulance was called. He was taken to Mountainside Hospital, where doctors discovered blood clots in both legs and near his heart. He was on a ventilator when I got there. I had time to hold his hand and tell him how much I loved him. I asked if he could hear me. He nodded, yes.

Crawford died of heart failure July 10, 2018 at 1:59 p.m. His daughter Keisha was in the room with me when he took his last breath. The two of us hugged. Our tears flowed. Doctors told me if Crawford had lived, both legs would have necessitated amputation.

Some 400 friends, family, and members of the Orange Police Department attended Crawford's funeral held at Bethel Baptist Church on Wallace Street in Orange, several blocks from his childhood home.

The small street was blocked off. Young women testified how his basketball programs changed their lives. He had inspired them to set goals, excel at whatever they chose to do in life and help others along the way. One male speaker at the funeral challenged other men in attendance to follow Crawford's example in caring for others and in working for the good of the community. Members of clubs he supported wore tee-shirts with Crawford's photo imprinted on them. I was overwhelmed.

I wrote personal letters to all those who attended the funeral. It took me almost a year. I wanted those friends to know how much it meant to me knowing that so many in Crawford's beloved hometown loved him as much as he loved them.

At the funeral, I was presented with a proclamation from Orange Mayor Dwayne D. Warren, Esq., "Honoring the Life and Legacy of Crawford Solon Daniels." Amazingly, the 13 "*WHEREAS*" statements tracked his entire life of giving.

*Rest in peace my brave warrior. I miss you so. But God promises we will meet again.*

## Stephen (Steve) D. Daniels

Stephen was born on September 24, 1949 in St. Elizabeth Hospital, Elizabeth, N. J. the same hospital where his brother, Crawford, was born two years earlier.

On the ride home from the hospital, I held Stephen in my arms. He was heavily swathed in blankets. In the back seat of our car, two-year-old Crawford seemed oblivious to the fact that a fourth human being was now part of the household. During the ride home that afternoon, Stephen made his presence known with a tiny whimper.

Crawford jumped up from the back seat of the car, looked over my shoulder, spotted the noisy creature and fell backwards onto his seat. He was silent the entire ride home.

Stephen was an even-tempered, good-natured child. He was musically and artistically inclined from an early age. At six years old, he drew Disney characters perfectly.

At Park Avenue Grade School, then nine years-old, Stephen played the flute-o-phone. "He plays the same notes as everyone else but *his* sound is much sweeter," his teacher told me. Stephen also played bass drum for the Orange High School Band and later toyed with trumpet lessons.

Growing up, Stephen found a kindred spirit in young Johnny Alston, another musically talented teen. They became best of friends, inseparable. Our home was Johnny's home.

Stephen surprised me one day, when at age 14, he announced he wanted to put his talents in music to use professionally. He was emphatic. "You've got to get me a set of drums, Mom. You've got to! I want to start a band!"

I was caught off guard by his request, despite being aware of his talents. I fussed all the way to the music store. "But you've never played drums!" I couldn't imagine how without having had lessons, he could be a successful drummer in a band that featured top 40 numbers.

Stephen got his drums, a gleaming psychedelic blue set. The rest is history.

Thankfully, residents in our neighborhood were forgiving of the sound of instruments piercing the air as the Dukes and Duchess band doggedly rehearsed. They quickly grew in popularity as I drove them from gig to gig, mostly night clubs. Money seemed to fall from the skies.

Eventually, the band became the Soul Dukes. One event sealed the band's popularity with a younger crowd.

An appearance by the Five Stairsteps, an up-and-coming group with a hit record, had been highly publicized for an outdoor concert in nearby Newark. Ironically, The Soul Dukes had rehearsed The Five Stairsteps' entire album and knew their songs well. The Five Stairsteps are remembered for such hits as "Come Back and "O-o-h Child."

"Mom, you've *got* to get us on that show!" Stephen pleaded.

From the urgency in his voice, I understood. This was *it. A chance to show their stuff at a big concert!*

I called the radio station that ran the ad for the event and asked for Hal Jackson. He was a well-known east coast disc jockey, and concert sponsor/promoter.

To my surprise, Jackson answered the phone. Again, to my surprise, he agreed to the Soul Dukes' appearance on the show.

Finally, it was showtime. The Soul Dukes were truly handsome in their spanking new purple outfits, purchased specifically for the event. They sat nervously on a corner of the stage, never dreaming how big their big moment would become!

Just before the concert was scheduled to start, Jackson appeared center stage, mike in hand, telling the young, restless crowd that the Five Stairsteps would *not be appearing*. We had no idea exactly why. We just learned they were stuck in Chicago.

Rumblings of discontent and disappointment started coming from the audience. Suddenly, Stephen yelled. "Hit it, Johnny!"

And Soul Dukes saxophonist Johnny Alston hit the stage with his sweet sax, singing the Stairsteps' hit song, "Come Back." There was a sudden quiet as the Soul Dukes band proceeded to perform several numbers from that album with as much skill, energy and expertise as the originators.

Hal Jackson was literally blown away. So was the crowd. And so was I.

*Here was God working in our lives again. When Stephen arrived and set up on stage, how could he ever have imagined that the Soul Dukes would actually be the Stars of the night.*

As the Soul Dukes mesmerized the crowd, Hal Jackson was backstage dumbstruck, asking over and over, *"Who is* that band? *Who is* that band?"

That night, a bond was forged with me, The Soul Dukes and Jackson. Later, Hal and his then wife, Alice tapped me to participate in their new venture, "Hal Jackson's Miss Black Teenage America" and later still, "Hal Jackson's Miss U.S Talented Teen" beauty pageant.

Jackson, who died May 23, 2012, became a storied businessman, having become part-owner of WLIB, a New York radio station and having produced his national beauty pageants. Also, in

1990, Jackson was the first minority inducted into the National Association of Broadcaster's Hall of Fame.

Meanwhile, over the years, Stephen's band went through several transformations evolving from The Dukes and Duchess, The Soul Dukes and, finally, Platinum Hook. A sterling reputation preceded them. They were on time. They were paid union wages and played Top 40 songs. They didn't stop between songs for breaks, playing a full 40 minutes every set. Club owners got their money's worth.

In fact, at one event the Soul Dukes performance so impressed an observer, he approached Stephen during a break.

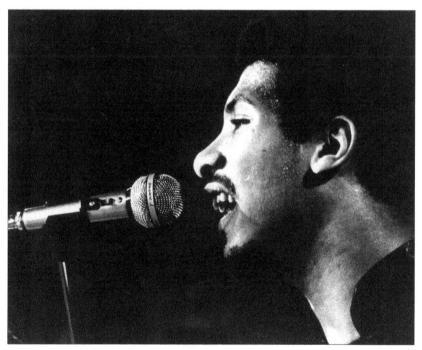

**Stephen sings**

"Who is your manager?" he asked Stephen "My mother," Stephen replied.

SOUL DUKES                    Jean Daniels, Mgr.
                              201-674-7025

That man happened to be George Hudson, a well-known impresario in the East Coast music world. He handed Stephen a card.

"Have her call me right away," he said." "I need a manager for
my new office."

I called George the next morning. He explained he recently
opened a radio ad agency and was seeking a manager for his firm.

"When I saw how regimented your group was, I was very impressed." George told me.

"Anyone who can manage a band with seven guys can certainly manage an office!" He later confessed he was startled when Stephen told him the Soul Dukes had a female manager.

I accepted the offer to manage George Hudson Associates, the first black-owned advertising agency in New Jersey.

*God was working in my life again! How else was it that my son's band is at a club, where their performance would attract someone in a position to offer me such a job?*

It was the beginning of many changes in my life.

Stephen was quick to jokingly remind me that *my* every success emanated from *his* first meetings with Hal Jackson and George Hudson. He used his 'launch of my career' argument as a bargaining point whenever he needed a favor.

His own success as band leader would be put to the test in the late 1960s. The Viet Nam War was raging, America's streets were aflame with protests against the war. And many young men were fleeing to Canada to avoid the draft.

One particular incident influenced me to try to keep my sons out of the Viet Nam War, if I could.

Stephen had graduated from Orange High School and was looking for a job. He applied for a position as a telephone lineman at New Jersey Bell Telephone Co. where I was employed at the time. He came home from that office rubbing his hands together triumphantly. The application included an aptitude test.

"Mom, I *know* I got the job! I knew the answers!"

But, several days later, he called the company for test results and was told that he failed the test. I called the company back, demanding to see the test.

"That's not possible," I was told.

I was so enraged I sat down and wrote a resignation letter to the New Jersey Bell president – but not before I secured another Job

"I refuse to work for a company that won't hire a young man who may one day have to defend this country," my letter to the president ended. Someone from the president's office called, offering to meet with me. I declined – something I regret to this day.

However, I became dead set against my sons serving in the hot, humid, jungles of Viet Nam. I encouraged Stephen and Crawford, both of whom were of age, to join the New Jersey National Guard in lieu of being drafted into the U. S. Army.

"If you can't get a decent job in your own country just because you're black, you don't go to war. If you fight in the Guard, at least it will be on our door steps," I reasoned to my sons.

Stephen and his brother signed up and were soon off to serving in the New Jersey National Guard.

Crawford wound up serving five years but, for Stephan, trouble loomed ahead.

Before leaving for duty, Stephen met with band members. All agreed that nothing would change in his absence. They would continue to work without him and get paid as usual, I would handle business as usual and, until he returned, the lead guitarist would be in charge.

But as soon as Stephen Left for training camp at Fort Leonard Wood, Mo., band members had other ideas.

They mutinied.

After their first job without Stephen, the band's "new" leader informed me: "Stephen is no longer our leader. We won't be returning the van."

I was stunned. What were they thinking? I had a full calendar of the band's engagements lined up, the details of which they knew nothing about. Plus, *I* owned the van.

I contacted Stephen at his base as quickly as I could. He arrived by flight in full uniform several days later. The Soul Dukes were playing at the Sterlington House in nearby Montclair. Stephen and I went straight there. The band was playing when we arrived.

I was so proud of Stephen. He was so handsome in his uniform and he handled himself so beautifully. We quietly took seats. Stephen sat straight of back, expressionless.

I felt his pain as he watched longtime school friends, his good buddies, betray him – and me. After all, hadn't I nurtured them through their teen years to this present moment? And hadn't I seen to it they got union wages for every performance, contributing greatly to their families' income? Stephen's best friend, Johnny Alston, was off to college and was not involved in this betrayal.

At the end of their set, Stephen calmly approached the band members. I don't know what was said. But he walked back to me. "They're going to bring the van back tomorrow," he said. We left as the band began playing their next set.

To this day, Stephen has never spoken a bitter word against his former buddies or surmised why the band took such action. It seems all has been forgiven. In fact, years later, former band members, some now in retirement, met at some point for a joyous reunion.

Meanwhile, on weekends from camp training, Stephen busied himself putting a new band together. I busied myself sending replacement bands to gigs for which the Soul Dukes had been booked. When the replacement bands worked, Stephen was paid his leader's pay even though he wasn't performing. Charles played with each replacement band and was paid as well.

But the economic winds of change were blowing. Local clubs were loath to hire eight-piece bands. Work was slow. I relinquished management of the band to a trusted promoter whose contacts were international.

So, when an opportunity to play an entire month in Mexico was presented, Stephen couldn't resist. It was an opportunity to keep members – all of whom relied on the band as their only source of income – working. He immediately approached his New Jersey lieutenants for permission to *temporarily* leave the state, to no avail.

Letters from me and a local minister attesting to the fact that the band was Stephen's business and band members' only source of income went ignored, were never considered.

**THE SOUL DUKES**

Manager
JEAN BRYANT
201-674-7025

"It's not fair, Stephen, complained. "The white boys ask for time off and they get it! I'm trying to keep my band working." He then asked my opinion about leaving the state.

"If you leave the state without permission, you're AWOL," I told him. "You will go to jail."

"If we don't have work, I'll lose the band," he opined.

It didn't take long for Stephen to make the decision to leave for Mexico. And it didn't take long for the FBI to get on Stephen's trail.

I had moved to Pittsburgh during this period and was working as Veterans Editor for the now defunct Pittsburgh press, when I got the disturbing call from my now ex-husband, Crawford:

"The band returned from Mexico," he informed me while I sat at my desk. "Stephen turned himself in! Your son is now in jail at Fort Dix!"

Crushed, dumbstruck, not knowing what to do, I learned back in my chair to ponder the situation – but only for a split second.

I actually had just interviewed Lt. Gen. Julius Becton Jr., who was black and serving at Fort Dix, a United States Army post in New Jersey!

Becton was in Pittsburgh for a speaking engagement at the University of Pittsburgh. As Press Veterans Editor, I was sent to cover the general for the story.

Suddenly, it hit me: While *I* was *interviewing the general* from Fort Dix here in Pittsburgh, Stephen was being *arrested* at Fort Dix, some 360 miles away!

*The inner force – God – was working again! Big time!*

I hurried to the Press Photo Department, where a picture of General Becton, taken at the University of Pittsburgh, was being developed.

"Blow up a picture of General Becton for me," I pleaded to photographer Don Stetzer, now deceased, explaining my urgency. I wanted a copy of Becton's picture to accompany the letter I was about to write him. An 8 x 10 photo would impress the general, I thought.

I nervously pounded the keys to my typewriter at my desk. The words seemed to flow easily as I explained why Stephen went AWOL: "Soul Dukes is an eight-member band that Stephen started at 14 years-old. Now, as young adults, it is their only livelihood," I wrote.

'Work for large bands was drying up." my letter continued. "For Stephen, not going to Mexico meant losing his band, the end of his dream. He *had* to leave, to go where the work was available...."

"Realizing the error of his ways, he turned himself in. Must a jail cell be his reward?" my letter ended.

In a few days, I heard from Stephen.

"Mom, I'm out!"

*What an awesome God we serve!*

After receiving my letter, Becton summoned Stephen to his office. Their meeting was brief, Stephen told me.

In the ensuing years, a less than robust economy and the rising popularity of well-equipped disc jockeys, dried up club work for live bands. In 2018 Platinum Hook, his new band, dissolved. Stephen found work as a drummer in an Italian wedding band and once did a stint backing up The Village People on drums on "The Tonight Show" with Jay Leno. Eventually, he found his niche in corporate management and gave up entertainment.

Meanwhile, as time went on, Stephen developed the need for a kidney. His wife and childhood sweetheart, Sheketa, was a match and donated hers.

*Praise God!*

However, because kidneys from a living donor usually only last between 10 and 13 years, Stephen found himself in need of a kidney once gain. Sadly, his compromised immune system could not withstand the long wait and he developed several illnesses – such as multiple myeloma and a perforated colon – that he could not overcome.

Stephen died October, 18, 2021, shortly after surgery in St. Barnabas, Hospital, Livingston N. J.

At his services in Memorial Funeral Home, Fanwood, N. J., I remembered how Stephen called me months before his death and blurted out:

"Mom, I miss my brothers!"

At the time, I had not considered those words an omen. But, as I stood at the bier of the casket gazing forlornly at my deceased son, I realized the weight those words carried.

Though I was deeply anguished at losing Stephen, it eased my soul to see so many of his former band mates come from near and far to Memorial Funeral Home in Fanwood, N. J. to express their love and say, "Farewell," to their former band leader.

The performance that members of the former Soul Dukes and Platinum Hook bands put together in a tribute to Stephen at his Home-Going service was priceless: Guitarist Robin Corley sang the words of the 23rd Psalm to a stunning arrangement.

How could they have known it's my favorite of the Book of Psalms, one my mother advised me years ago to find solace in during times of stress and sorrow.

*Thank you, God, for such an unexpected gift!*

Stephen and Sheketa brought five children to their marriage. Her children are Ronald and Burton Henson. Stephen's children are daughters Brooke Daniels Gillespie and Taylor Daniels and a son, Stephen C. Daniels.

*I miss you, my son. I believe the music you make in Heaven will be sweeter than everyone else's*

## Bernard J. Daniels

Bernard was born September 28, 1951 in Orange Memorial Hospital, Orange, N.J. He was named Bernard after his maternal great-grandfather and James after his paternal grandfather.

Growing up, Bernard was rather quiet. Through his high school years, he worked part-time in his father's auto body shop and became a skilled auto body repairman.

He had no interest in college basically because of the expertise and joy he found in auto repair, His dream was to follow his dad in business. We looked forward to his upcoming graduation from Orange High School.

How could we know that graduation day, June 15, 1969 – at Orange High School would be the beginning of a nightmare for Bernard and our family. As we watched him proudly receive his high school diploma at the graduation ceremony that evening at Orange High School, we could not have imagined that what should have been a time of joyousness would wind up being a time of horror.

Immediately after the program, family members shared congratulatory hugs with Bernard. He left us and went on to join other graduates at local parties.

But about 1:00 a.m. that morning, I was awakened by a phone call from a frightened woman. I couldn't identify the voice and she didn't identify herself.

I answered, steeled for bad news.

"Two cops arrested your son," she said hurriedly. "They said he was speeding! They threw him in their car for no reason! He was polite to them. Oh, hurry!" Her voice was shaking with fear.

Without calling anyone, I sped to the Orange Police Station in my station wagon. I was too late. The desk sergeant had already released Bernard without charges to the disappointment of the two officers, who proceeded to follow Bernard as he left the station for his car.

Before I could get to him, the two rogue cops had already ordered Bernard back into their car and driven him several blocks to St. John's Church graveyard, where they beat him with blackjacks and taunted him, saying, "We want to see how tough you are."

I found him limping, sobbing, trying to make it back to his car. I was hysterical, horrified, seeing my son in this condition. I parked my car alongside the road, got out and took him into my arms. I tried to comfort him as he stood trembling from his beating.

I drove as fast as I could several blocks to nearby Orange Memorial Hospital, where he received treatment for swellings on his left arm and left leg. After an hour, he was released.

When we left the hospital, I told Bernard we could leave his car where it was and pick it up later. But he insisted on driving it home. I tailed him all the way in case the two rogue cops were still on the prowl.

How traumatic it was for Bernard. How painful for this mother not to have been there to save her son.

At home, I phoned the police station, screaming about what happened. The desk sergeant listened patiently and said there would be an investigation.

I was outraged over the audacity of those rogue cops. How dare they perpetrate an atrocity on my son, a child, who was *taught* to believe police were our protectors.

And just two years earlier, Bernard's oldest brother, Crawford, had suffered horrifically at the hands of Newark police.

It took these horrid experiences to awaken me from the bourgeoisie existence I had been living; My business-owner husband and I owned two homes, two cars. He allotted me a generous allowance to run the household. I had truly believed what we taught our children – that the police are here to protect, to do no harm.

Later that day, still in a rage, I had one mission – to get justice for Bernard. I typed and mailed letters to every church, synagogue and newspaper in Orange and neighboring towns about "the atrocity perpetrated against my son at the hands of Orange Police."

I tried to file atrocious assault and battery charges against the officers, but the clerk, (who had the same last name as one of the officers) reduced the charges to simple assault and battery.

I then went to the St. John's church, hoping to find indignation from members and leaders that their church grounds were used by police for such a vicious crime.

I found no such thing.

When I knocked on the church door, I expected the church secretary. I was surprised to see a man in black robes. I assumed he was a priest. I began explaining who I was and why I was there, when he gruffly cut me off.

"Get out of here!" he snarled.

I was left standing in disbelief as the church door closed in my face. My head was spinning. What? No welcome? No compassion? This from a man of God?

On the other hand, leaders of other churches and synagogues flooded my mailbox with replies to my earlier letters regarding Bernard's plight. All were sympathetic, wanting to know how they could be of help. I wasn't sure how to respond at the time. Things were happening so fast. We were proceeding through the court system and our case was now before a Grand jury.

Despite news stories, there was no public outcry in the community about Bernard's mistreatment by police. While disappointing, I understood the hesitancy. Many found it hard to believe such a terrible thing could happen at the hands of police. They believed that Bernard must have brought it upon himself.

Those thoughts quickly changed several months later when Orange Police were at it again.

After leaving a local tavern, three Orange Police officers, harassed and physically attacked 17-year-old Rosalind Lewis as she walked her dog because she voiced objection to the racist remarks they shouted at her. As if that wasn't enough, the cops shot and killed the dog. They also threatened the girl's mother who came to her daughter's rescue.

In the meantime, our case wound through the court system and before a grand jury. But the outcome was not in our favor. The two cops who beat Bernard were acquitted.

I cried unashamedly. On the way out of the courtroom, the two thug cops passed by me, mocking my sobs. "Boo Hoo, Boo Hoo," they gleefully said in unison.

"Cut that out!" The judge admonished them.

When Bernard saw the open disrespect the two cops had for me, he begged me to end his case. "Mom I'm alright now. I don't want to go to court anymore, he pleaded. I wanted to continue fighting for justice for him. But I also knew my son, how fragile his temperament was, that he had already been through enough.

I became a member of an advisory board to the Orange Bureau of Police Human Relations department but did not serve long as I left for Pittsburgh soon after.

Tragically, six years would pass and the suffering of many more Orange citizens would occur at the hands of some of the Orange police before there would be any accountability – in a sense.

On March 25, 1975 two top Orange Police officials and 16 others were indicted for such offenses as fraud, hindering an investigation for illegal gambling and quashing tickets. However, none were indicted for brutality against Orange citizenry.

Ironically, some years later, Bernard's older brother, Crawford, joined the Orange Police force. This move was not without opposition from the department's upper echelon, who considered him radical because of his community activism.

However, Bernard soldiered on in his life and continued to work with his father but he was never the same. Tragically, at one point, he turned to drugs. Later, he was diagnosed with colon cancer. The cancer was already in advanced stages, so was incurable.

I brought Bernard from New Jersey to live with me in Pittsburgh during his illness. He was proud of my work with youths, particularly the Mister African American program.

"When I first saw those young men in their tuxedoes, I wanted to cry," he told me the first time he attended a MAA show.

I treasured Bernard's comment, hoping the audience felt the same wave of emotion at seeing the young black men so handsome in such a positive setting.

Bernard lived with me five years before he died August 26, 1999, in Montefiore Hospital in Pittsburgh's Oakland section. That night, three dear friends – Penny Walker, Josie Hatley and Gwen Moore – sat with me in his hospital room so I wouldn't be alone as Bernard took his last breaths. I lifted him slightly and held him in my arms. My tears fell on his face as he began slipping away.

With great difficulty, Bernard managed to whisper his last words to me.

"Mom, why are you crying?"

I held him tighter, "Because I'm losing you." I answered sobbing. And I released Bernard, my third son and the first to pass away to God.

*Rest in Peace my brave and courageous soldier. According to God's Word, we will meet again. I live for that moment.*

# Ode To Bernard

*By His Mother, Jean Bryant*

Bernard, what *words* can convey my lonliness
for you so that others understand?

For *words* are so fleeting as though written in the sand.

No, there are no *words* to describe
this mother's bleeding heart.

*Words* disappear too quickly just as
we were made to part.

But still my son, I know though
you're no longer in my sight,

My tears speak more than *words,*
of the sadness I feel each night

So, I won't expect that *words* can tell others of my pain

Instead, I'll let my tears keep falling just like drops of rain.

And I'll go to sleep each night remembering
how I held you in my arms

As God called you to come home so you'd be
protected from all harm

So, my dear, I realize more than ever that my tears

Really speak words of joy for all the happy years.

And now, as the years go slowly by,

My tears reflect those times we shared,

Just you, Bernard, and I.

## Charles C. Daniels

Charles Clinton Daniels arrived in this world on June 30, 1953 in Orange Memorial Hospital. He was named after my Uncle Charles Wilmore, the first African-American postman in my home town, Roselle, N. J. His middle name, Clinton, was after my step-dad, Clinton Williams.

Charles was born a day before my birthday, July 1. He was often kidded about being my birthday present. By the age of three, Charles was exhibiting a great sense of humor. He was good at mimicking people and relished the attention it got him.

My most vivid memory of his playfulness is of him mocking the hunchback in the classic movie, "The Hunchback of Notre Dame." We watched it on television one afternoon when he was three. The hunchback was a pathetic, disfigured character who also limped. When the movie was over, Charles jumped off the couch and pulled the rim of his right eye downward.

He looked at me for approval as he danced around mocking the movie character. I tried not to laugh but it was just too funny. I did stop him, however, because I didn't want him to ruin his eye. And, although the Hunchback character was fictional, I didn't want Charles to grow up making fun of people with real disabilities.

Charles was the apple of his father's eye. He learned early on to use his father's loving attention to his advantage, to get treats or permission to go places. But, being a favored child was not enough to prevent Charles from undergoing a radical change during his middle school years.

Starting with his pre-teen years, he underwent a change in personality. He stopped going to school. He was only 14 years old. His father and I tried everything we could to turn this around, to get him interested in the learning process again. Nothing worked.

He did, however, enjoy being around his dad's autobody shop. With misgivings, we relented and allowed Charles to do small jobs around the shop.

Eventually, Crawford Sr. opened a second shop in partnership with a white friend, "Ned." (A fictitious name is being used for purposes of privacy). That shop, in nearby Montclair, was much busier than the shop near our Ward Street home.

Crawford Sr. sent Charles to the new shop to do small chores and occasionally pump gas. In the course of his duties, Charles noticed a strange woman making daily visits to the shop, sometimes at breakfast time, sometimes at lunch time.

Charles told his father and me about it. "She bosses me a lot," he said.

Crawford had already sensed something was wrong there. For the amount of traffic and body work at the shop, it wasn't producing the money it should have been.

So, one day, we high tailed it to the shop. We arrived – unannounced – just before closing. I took over the receipts of the day, tallying them on an old adding machine, while Crawford confronted "Ned" in the bay area.

It didn't take me long to realize that the cash in the drawer did not match the amount that should have been there based on the day's receipts. It was quite apparent that a substantial amount of money was missing. When I tallied the receipts of several days against bank deposits, they didn't compute either. It was obvious that money was being siphoned off, not being deposited to the business.

This finding did not sit well with Crawford and the two men were soon trading blows. Frightened, I tried not to hear the sound of thuds being landed as the two men fought.

Oddly, "Ned" never tried to defend himself about the missing money. We knew "Ned's" wife, but didn't know who the mystery woman was. What we also didn't know was where the missing money went. Since the business was so new, we decided to dissolve the partnership, cut our losses, walk away.

As Charles grew older, he developed a rich, golden voice that thrilled Miss Black Teenage contestants in Pittsburgh. Charles' crowd pleaser was his soulful rendition of Joe Cocker's "You Are So" Beautiful."

From 1975 on, Charles serenaded contestants each year, while they stood on stage as a group. He sang before finalists were announced. The message was clear, no matter who was crowned winner or runner-up, they were all beautiful.

At 18, Charles became a full-fledged member of his brother Stephen's band of new members, which was then under new management. And Charles was content traveling the East Coast as the Soul Dukes' bongo player and sometime vocalist.

When the opportunity arose for the band to travel to Mexico, I had my doubts about Charles traveling there. Quite frankly, I didn't want him to go. At 18, I believed he was still too impressionable. He appealed to his dad, who overrode me and Charles had his way.

The night before the band left for Mexico, I had a serious talk with them about being in a strange country, about obeying the laws of the land, about staying away from drugs or drug users and about the long sentences foreigners could get for disobeying laws.

So, away they went. At the end of the month-long gig at a popular club, the house band threw a party for The Soul Dukes. As fate would have it, Mexican police raided the party. I learned later, that they were looking for the house band's female member.

It was told to me that the young singer was having an affair with the club owner and that she was becoming a problem for him. Unknown to Charles, the club owner set-up the raid to rid himself of his "problem."

Unfortunately, Charles made a fateful attempt to try to save the girl and got caught in the web of a wicked plot.

He took her stash of marijuana and attempted to hide it on his person. Everybody was searched. When he was searched, the stash was found. He was arrested and jailed at the former infamous Lecumberri Prison in Mexico City, a prison with a notorious past reputation for torture and murder of its prisoners.

Charles experienced none of that and the prison no longer exists. The building was turned over to the National Archive in 1980 after being decommissioned as a prison four years earlier.

Meanwhile, Stephen called to let me know what happened. He assured me that Charles was okay. He had visited him at Lecumberri. Charles was unharmed. The main thing he needed – and fast – was money for a lawyer, Stephen stressed.

I was hysterical. My baby son was in a foreign prison with a horrendous reputation. I felt helpless.

*But that Inner Force –God – stepped in.*

I snapped out of despair and into action. I hurriedly wrote to then U. S. Sen. Hugh Scott, (R- PA) in Washington, D. C. and to the U.S. consulate in Mexico City, complaining that the plight of American Citizens was being ignored at the prison. I also prevailed upon a lawyer-friend to pay a visit to Mexico City on Charles' behalf.

Sen. Scott, now deceased, contacted the U.S. consulate in Mexico and got assurances that Charles' case was being reviewed. Representatives of the Consulate claimed to have visited Charles twice, Scott wrote me. Later, my lawyer friend returned from Mexico City with helpful information. Charles was being held *without* charges or *without* a court date, which he told me was unusual.

As weeks turned into months, Charles seemed to accept his fate for however long it lasted, an attitude you would expect from a much older man. He was visited by several Mexican lawyers asking for money but promising nothing. Also, some of the money I sent Charles never reached him and he had suspicions about who might be stealing it.

All these worries took its toll on me. I began to have nightmares, imagining what might be happening to Charles that he dared not confide in his letters or in phone calls.

Months rolled by. It soon became apparent that getting Charles out of prison would not be an easy task. The family rallied. His father, his brother Crawford and I made separate trips to Mexico to see Charles and to meet with lawyers to no avail. I deduced that they all must have looked into the case and, for some reason, decided not to touch it.

Finally, John Troan, editor at the Pittsburgh Press, became aware of Charles' situation through the office grapevine. A gentle, kind man, Troan, now deceased, quietly approached me at my desk.

"Jean, I'm sorry about your son," Troan began. "Let's see if I can be of some help." Troan said he met and befriended then United Press International manger Denny Davis at a conference in Mexico City.

"I've already talked to Denny about your son and he's willing to look into the matter. Give him a call and keep me posted," Troan said. Sensing my sadness, he smiled, patted me on the shoulder and went back to his office.

From that point, maneuvers began that would eventually set Charles on the path to freedom.

*That constant Force – God – was at work again.*

When I called Denny in Mexico City and explained Charles' situation, he promised to "get right on it. I'll make a list of any expenses I incur. I'll be spending my own money so I'll need compensation."

I felt good about that phone call. Denny seemed like a man of action, a straight talker, a man of his word.

*God is showing up again!*

A letter to me from Charles dated December 19, 1973, advised me that Denny had visited him. Charles wrote nothing about their conversation, however.

But Denny's frequent phone calls to me revealed that he was working feverishly with various factions, including the American Embassy, to get the ball rolling for Charles' release.

He confirmed there were no charges against Charles, nor had a court date been scheduled for him.

Months later, on March 11, 1974, I got an unexpected call from Denny.

"I just put Charles on a plane to Chicago. And he was mighty happy to be going home!" Denny exclaimed, adding that a connecting flight would bring Charles to Pittsburgh later that day. He explained that once Charles' release was confirmed there was no time to waste, no time to call me in advance. It was just "Go!"

My heart seemed to be beating out of my chest at the news! I was overcome with joy. My baby son was coming home to me, to his family, to the United States! I notified Troan, expressing my thanks for his part in Charles' release.

I called New Jersey – my mother, Charles' dad, Stephen, my sister, Sarah and my twin sister, Betty in Oslo, Norway. We all rejoiced at the news of Charles' release.

In all, Charles spent two years at Lecumberri prison *without charges* and *without a court hearing*.

When Dewey and I met Charles at Pittsburgh International Airport, he was deliriously happy. He told us how he kissed the ground in Chicago when he deplaned there. Charles settled in with us on Beldale Street and easily adapted to life in Pittsburgh.

A few months later, my Pittsburgh Press colleague Mike Anderson wrote of Charles' Mexico experience. The article distressed my mother who felt that this part of Charles' life should have remained private. She was concerned that public knowledge would cause him to be scorned and denied job opportunities.

"You've ruined his life," she said to me after reading the account. She was wrong.

It didn't ruin Charles' life after all. In fact, Anderson's account was instrumental in Charles getting a job with the Gulf Oil Corporation. Roy Kohler, then Public Relations director at Gulf's Downtown headquarters, contacted me after reading about Charles' misfortune and scheduled a job interview. There was an immediate opening in Gulf's mailroom. And Charles was hired.

*God showed up again! What an awesome God!*

The ensuing years in Pittsburgh were largely uneventful for Charles. He was helpful to me during my divorce from Dewey Bryant. When we moved to our newly purchased home in Stanton Heights, Charles busied himself summers planting a garden of tomatoes, in which he took great pride.

Charles was an animal lover and took great care of Max, a cat he rescued when our neighbor entered a nursing home, and Wolfe, a husky he named when he found the dog abandoned in our neighborhood.

In mid-2014, Charles was diagnosed with stage-four prostate cancer. The news threw him. But he vowed to fight it with all his might. After a courageous five-year battle, Charles succumbed on July 18, 2019.

Against my wishes, Charles insisted on being cremated. I acted accordingly. A memorial was held for him on July 26, 2019 at White Memorial Chapel, in Wilkinsburg.

*I miss you, my baby son. The beautiful sunsets you often watched and captured on camera. Yes, they miss you too.*

## Charlie's Quatrain & All That Jazz

Head thrown back prankster' jest
Leather sack 'cross his chest
Motor bike sunny day
Freedom ride float away
S'liberty Mexico
Jersey pageant show
bongo drums heart beat song
guitar strums love lasts long
Nature's friend o'er the years
earth shall tend fallen tears
pensive face inner world
private space sanctum furled
Mother's twin for awhile
let us in share a smile
brother man child of moon
slipped from clan gone too soon
understand not the end
take my hand meet again

*by Susan P. Johnson*
*LOVE U BROTHER*

At Pittsburgh Black Media Federation event

Chapter Seven:

# My Awards

**My Professional & Community Awards**

**Talk Magazine Salute To – 1974**
*Black Achievers*

**Youth Motivation Task Force – June 25, 1976**
*"Dedicated Work That Shines Like a Guiding Light
Along a Path for Our Youth"*

**Iota /Phi Lamda Sorority-Pi Chapter – April 26, 1980**
*"Woman of the Year"*

**Bon Ami Temple #49 – 1984**
*Meritorious Service In the Community*

**Jefferson Award – January 1985**

**The Pittsburgh Black Media Federation –
Robert L. Vann Award – 1985**
*"Journalistic Excellence"*

**The Pittsburgh Black Media Federation -
Robert L. Vann Award -1987**
*Print/Feature: "Standing Out"*

**YWCA Of Greater Pittsburgh Leadership Award**
*Communications*

**Women In Communication Matrix Award – April 21, 1987**
*Honorble Mention – News Series, "Power Struggle"*

**Operation Dig/Careers, Inc. – June 13, 1987**
*"Humanitarian Work"*

**Golden Quill Award – 1987**
*Daily Newspaper: Enterprise Investigative Finalist*

**Keystone Press Award, Div I; Pa Newspaper Publishers'**
**Assoc.– The Pittsburgh Press – DIV. I. Daily – 1987**
*"Excellence in Journalism; News Series, Second Place"*

**Pittsburgh Young Adult Club/Nanbpw Clubs, Inc. – 1987**

**Champions Association/Sly Jock – 1990**

**First Annual Little Miss Afro-American Pageant Award – 1991**
*In Appreciation for Your Dedication and Support*

**Sheridan Broadcasting Corporation Award – 1995**
*Community Service*

**Renaissance Publications Trail Blazer – 1998**
*"Youth Empowerment"*

**The Pittsburgh Black Media Federation – 1999**
*Distinguished Service Award"*

**WAMO Radio – 1995**
*Best Reporter – Print*

**New Pittsburgh Courier - 2006**
*50 Women of Influence Award*

**Pittsburgh Black Media Federation – 2007**
*Legends In Journalism – Print Pioneer*

**New Pittsburgh Courier – 2008**
*50 Women of Excellence Award*

**Cribs for Kids – 2010**
*Women of Achievement- Young Women's Advocate*

**The New Pittsburgh Courier 50 Women of Excellence – 2012**
*Legacy Award Honoree*

**Rankin/Mon Valley/Pittsburgh, PA Section**

**National Counil of Negro Women, Inc. – 2013**
*Legacy Award*

**Inducted In Pittsburgh Fashion Hall of Fame – 2013**
*September 29,2013 William Penn Hotel, Downtown*

Jeff Gray attends ceremony honoring Jean Bryant and several others at Heinz Hall, Downtown Pittsburgh. The event was hosted by stage and screen star Tamara Tunie, a former Miss Black teenage contestant.

# Chapter Eight:

# Acknowledgements

*My Thanks To:*

Miss Black Teenage /Mister African Committee Members

For their dedication to Teenagers during their most critical years:

Bea Mitchell and Anthony Mitchell

Betty Moore

Brenda Simons

Carmella Cheatham

Carolyn Toney and Willie Toney

Charlene Grigsby

Flora White

Crystal Woodward

Charlene Grigsby

Connie McDaniel and Kimberly Mc Daniel Lightfoot

Debra Humphries

Earlina Williams and Veronica Williams

Edna Rhodes

Francis Samuels

Gwen Moore and George Moore and Renee Moore

Jean Anderson and Anthony Anderson and **Maya**

Jeannine McKelvia and Jamel McKelvia

Josephine Hatley and Elbert Hatley

Kevin Smith

LaMont Jones Jr.

Lonita Ross

Madelyn Smith

Meta McMillian

Minister Synthia Sweptson

Penny Turner

Penny Walker and Donna Walker

Ronald B. Saunders

Verna Johnson

Wayne and Toni Phinisee

**Thanks Also To:**

**Chris Moore and Joyce Meggerson-Moore**, for their continued financial support of the Miss Black Teenage/ Mister African American programs and for their continuing friendship

**Annette Banks WQED-TV**, Producer, for her EMMY award winning video, "Crowning Achievement," a story about my work with pageantry and for her continuing friendship

**Carl Truss and Richard Gillcrese** for their excellent videography over the years and for their continuing friendship

**Minette Seate, WQED Senior Producer**, for suggesting my profile for the 2020 Black History Month

**Carolyn Callahan** and **Earlina Williams** for their steadfast friendship and helpfulness during my time of disability

**Connie Portis**, for her support of my endeavors and for her continuing friendship

**Glenn and Andrea Mahone** for his early corporate sponsorship of the Miss Black Teenage Program and for both their support in my community endeavors as President of the Stanton Heights Community Organization and for their continuing friendship

**Macedonia Baptist Church**, Pastor Brian Edmonds, for his inspirational messages

**Pastor Archie D. Perrin and Perrin Family**, for their support of the Mister African American Program and Miss Black Teenage Pageant

**Sandra Ward and Lydia Francis**, for their help, love and caring for Charles in his waning days

**James L. Rice Owner/Operator**, 13 McDonald restaurants, for his support and his important lecture to Mister African American participants

**James Mc Donald**, for his many years of support and donations for the Miss Black teenage Pageant and for his continuing friendship

**Traci Mc Donald**, for initiating and securing four-year tuition-free scholarships to Clarion University for the MBT/MAA programs and her continuing friendship

**Gemma Stemley**, for also securing four-year tuition-free scholarships to Clarion University for the MBT/MAA programs and for her continuing friendship

**Vivienne Robinson**, for her continuous support for my endeavors and for her continuing friendship

**Zilla Thompson**, for her lectures to MBT contestants and for her continuing friendship

# Chapter Nine

# Jean's Favorite God Story

It happened many years ago on an extremely hot morning. I was on my way to work when I stopped for a red light at the corner of Commonwealth and Liberty Downtown near the then Hilton Hotel.

The light changed. I started to drive on but the motor suddenly quit. I turned the key. The motor just groaned. I couldn't roll down the windows or unlock the doors. The locks had been sawed down to deter thieves, I couldn't pull them up. I couldn't even blow the horn. Everything was electrical.

I was trapped! I panicked. Hoping to attract attention, I beat on the driver side window with my fists. But passing drivers only gaped at me. No one stopped.

I was sweating profusely. Inside, the car seemed to get smaller and smaller, hotter and hotter. I could hardly breathe. I panicked and beat on the windshield with all my might. Again, no one stopped. No one seemed to understand what was happening to me.

But *J. R., of Oakdale, did. *(*Initials are being used for purposes of privacy*).

Driving off the Parkway's Boulevard of the Allies Exit ramp with his wife, Joan, now deceased, J. R. swerved his car off the ramp into traffic to get to me. He cut off some drivers. Horns were blasting, drivers were yelling at him.

"A lady's in trouble," I heard him yell.

J. R. parked his car and raced to me. "What's wrong," he asked through the car window as a small crowd began to gather.

"I can't get out. Nothing's working," I cried

"I'm not going to leave you. We'll get you some help," J. R. promised.

Meanwhile, the growing crowd caught the attention of a man cutting grass on Point State Park grounds across the street from where I sat entrapped. He shut down his lawn mower and slowly ambled over to check out the situation. He pressed through the growing crowd, peered into my car, dug into his pants pocket and pulled out a small flat instrument.

"I'm going to get you out," the Lawn Man said. "Take your car key off the ring." My hands were shaking terribly but I managed to do it.

"I'm going to pull the top of the window window open just a little," he said. "Slip the key through to me." I did as I was directed. The Lawn Man caught my key and quickly unlocked the passenger door.

Finally, my terrible ordeal was over.

How did J. R. spot me from his moving vehicle almost a half-block away? How was he so moved to intervene and help me when others kept going? What made the Lawn Man stop working and cross the street to see what was happening?

*God placed J. R. and the Lawn Man in my path.*

I truly believe if J. R. or the Lawn Man had not intervened, I might have suffocated.

J. R., now 90 years old, cannot recall the exact date of the incident. But he remembers it well.

"What an interesting morning that was," J. R. wrote me recently. "A lady in distress and a couple in the right place at the right time. Could it have worked out any better? I don't think so."

# Chapter Ten

# Jean's Favorite Basic Recipe for Pancakes

**Sift together:**

| | |
|---|---|
| 2 | cups flour |
| ⅛ | teaspoon salt |
| 4 | teaspoons baking powder |
| 2 | Tablespoons white sugar |

Cut in with a fork or other device: 4 Tablespoons softened butter until mixture is crumbly

**Add:**

| | |
|---|---|
| 1¼ | cup 2 pct milk (A little at a time with |
| 2 | eggs, mixed gently) |

Grease griddle, heat to 350 degrees. Cook 3 min, or until bubbles occur, turn pancake over, cook 3 minutes or until done.

**Note: if mixture is too thick, add more milk a little at a time until right consistency, not too thick, not too thin.

Yield: About 8 pancakes

## Chapter Eleven
# Jean's Favorite Creed

*"I expect to pass through life but once*
*If, therefore, there be any kindness I can show, or*
*Any good thing I can do for any fellow being,*
*Let me do it now and not defer or neglect it…*
*As I shall not pass this way again"*

Ralph Waldo Emerson